2013/14 Edition

# OCR
# AS Biology
# Unit 1
# Revision Workbook

Samantha Richardson

# The Revision Academy

The company provides specialised revision that is specific to each exam within the following exam boards:
- AQA
- EDEXCEL
- OCR
- WJEC

We pride ourselves on attention to detail when it comes to revising and ensure that different learning styles are catered for.
The company currently delivers the following to help boost candidates grades:
- Workbooks specific to each individual exam
- One to one private tutoring sessions
- Intensive small group revision days specific to particular exams

For more information on these services visit our website at www.therevisionacademy.co.uk.

Samantha Richardson, a fully qualified Teacher, started the company in 2008. She has had many successes with her pupils since then and the company has grown steadily.
Samantha has a Masters degree from the University of Southampton and a Post Graduate Certificate of Education from the University of Cambridge. She has worked in both state and private schools and held the position of Head of Science before founding The Revision Academy.

Published by:
Synthus
29 Hickory Lane
Almondsbury
Bristol
BS32 4FR
UK                www.synthus.co.uk/publishing

© The Revision Academy 2013

First printed 2013
ISBN 978-1-910060-02-5
All rights reserved. No part of this publication may be reproduced, stored in a retrieval system, or transmitted in any form or by any means, electronic, mechanical, photocopying, recording or otherwise, without the prior permission of the Publisher or a licence permitting restricted copying in the United Kingdom issued by the Copyright Licensing Agency, Saffron House, 6-10 Kirby Street, London EC 1N 8TS.

This workbook has been written specifically to support students preparing for the OCR Specification AS Biology F211 examination. The content has been neither approved nor endorsed by OCR and remains the sole responsibility of the author.

# About this book

The book contains many different revision techniques to help support you when preparing for the unit 1 exam.

The first section aims to check and test all of your basic knowledge of each topic. Here you should try to include all the key words and terms as they are vital to attaining full marks in exam questions.

The second section gives you space to keep all of your key notes on the most difficult topics of the module.

The third section highlights which subjects have been included in past papers so you may easily access questions on particular topics and give you a possible feel for what may come up in your exam.

The fourth section contains longer questions that require knowledge of several topics and how they are linked together.

The fifth section gives you examples of flow diagrams of all the key processes of the module.

The sixth section gives a list of the key concepts of the module that you can use to complete memory spider diagrams to check your current knowledge.

Finally the answers to all the basic questions and linked topic questions are included.

# Contents

## Basic Questions — 7
Microscopy — 8
Cells and their contents — 12
Membranes & Transport — 20
Water — 27
Cell Cycles & Divisions — 31
Organism Organisation — 38
Exchange & the Lungs — 41
Transport in Animals — 46
Transport in Plants — 60

## Smart Notes — 75

## Past Paper Contents — 89

## Linked Topic Questions — 93

## Flow Diagrams — 99

## Memory Spider Diagram Topics — 119

## Answers — 121
Microscopy — 122
Cells and their contents — 123
Membranes & Transport — 125
Water — 126
Cell Cycles & Divisions — 127
Organism Organisation — 128
Exchange & the Lungs — 129
Transport in Animals — 131
Transport in Plants — 134
Linked Topic Question Answers — 137

## Acknowledgements — 139
Also in this series....... — 140

# Basic Questions

This section contains questions on the basic knowledge you will need to know for each topic of the exam.

These questions are useful to answer a few times through your revision. We recommend you do them the first time using your text books and notes to help you and then answer them a second time using less help.

You can order additional copies of the questions by contacting us at info@therevisionacademy.co.uk.

BASIC QUESTIONS

# Microscopy

The OCR specification states the following learning outcomes for microscopes:

**Candidates should be able to:**

(1) **State** the resolution and magnification that can be achieved by a light microscope, a transmission electron microscope and a scanning electron microscope;

(2) **Explain** the difference between magnification and resolution;

(3) **Explain** the need for staining samples for use in light microscopy and electron microscopy;

(4) **Calculate** the linear magnification of an image (HSW3);

(5) **Describe and interpret** drawings and photographs of eukaryotic cells as seen under an electron microscop and be able to recognise the following structures: nucleus, nucleolus, nuclear envelope, rough and smooth endoplasmic reticulum (ER), Golgi apparatus, ribosomes mitochondria, lysosomes, chloroplasts, plasma (cell surface) membrane, centrioles, flagella and cilia

# Microscopy

1. What do the following terms mean:

   **Magnification -**

   ..................................................................................................................................

   ..................................................................................................................................

   **Resolution -**

   ..................................................................................................................................

   ..................................................................................................................................

2. What is **staining**?

   ..................................................................................................................................

   ..................................................................................................................................

   ..................................................................................................................................

3. What is **sectioning**?

   ..................................................................................................................................

   ..................................................................................................................................

   ..................................................................................................................................

4. How do you calculate **total magnification**?

   ..................................................................................................................................

   ..................................................................................................................................

5. What are the resolutions for:

   **Human eye -**

   ..................................................................................................................................

   ..................................................................................................................................

**Light microscope -**

..................................................................................................................................
..................................................................................................................................

**Electron microscope**

..................................................................................................................................
..................................................................................................................................

6. How do you measure cells seen in a microscope?

..................................................................................................................................
..................................................................................................................................
..................................................................................................................................

7. How is an **eye piece graticule** calibrated?

..................................................................................................................................
..................................................................................................................................
..................................................................................................................................
..................................................................................................................................
..................................................................................................................................
..................................................................................................................................

8. What is the equation for calculating actual size of an object?

..................................................................................................................................
..................................................................................................................................

9. How does an **electron microscope** work?

..................................................................................................................................
..................................................................................................................................
..................................................................................................................................
..................................................................................................................................

10. What is the difference between a **scanning electron microscope** and a **transmission electron microscope**?

　

11. What are the advantages and disadvantages of **electron microscopes**?

　

12. What are the benefits of using colour **electron micrographs**?

　

13. What are the similarities and differences of **light microscopes** and **electron microscopes**?

# Cells and their contents

The OCR specification states the following learning outcomes for cells and their contents:

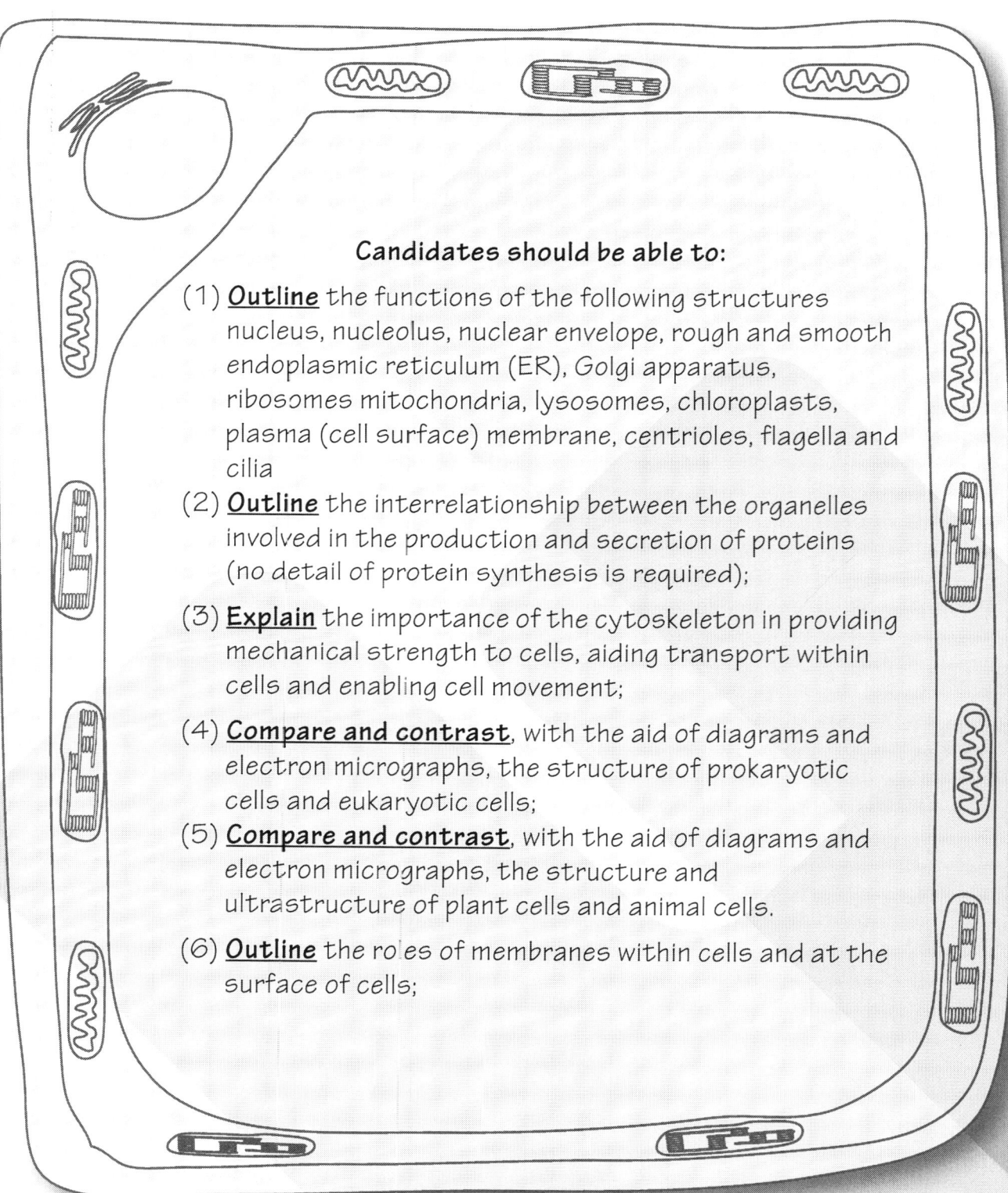

**Candidates should be able to:**

(1) **Outline** the functions of the following structures nucleus, nucleolus, nuclear envelope, rough and smooth endoplasmic reticulum (ER), Golgi apparatus, ribosomes mitochondria, lysosomes, chloroplasts, plasma (cell surface) membrane, centrioles, flagella and cilia

(2) **Outline** the interrelationship between the organelles involved in the production and secretion of proteins (no detail of protein synthesis is required);

(3) **Explain** the importance of the cytoskeleton in providing mechanical strength to cells, aiding transport within cells and enabling cell movement;

(4) **Compare and contrast**, with the aid of diagrams and electron micrographs, the structure of prokaryotic cells and eukaryotic cells;

(5) **Compare and contrast**, with the aid of diagrams and electron micrographs, the structure and ultrastructure of plant cells and animal cells.

(6) **Outline** the roles of membranes within cells and at the surface of cells;

# Cells and their contents

1. What is an **organelle**?

   ..................................................................................................
   ..................................................................................................
   ..................................................................................................

2. What is an **ultra structure**?

   ..................................................................................................
   ..................................................................................................
   ..................................................................................................

3. What are the roles of the following:

   **Cytoskeleton -**

   ..................................................................................................
   ..................................................................................................

   **Flagella -**

   ..................................................................................................
   ..................................................................................................

   **Vesicles & Vacuoles -**

   ..................................................................................................
   ..................................................................................................

   **Plant cell walls -**

   ..................................................................................................
   ..................................................................................................

BASIC QUESTIONS

4. What are the structures and functions of the following:

**Nucleus -**

**Endoplasmic reticulum -**

**Golgi apparatus -**

**Mitochondria -**

**Chloroplasts -**

**Lysosomes -**

**Ribosomes -**

..................................................................................................................................

..................................................................................................................................

..................................................................................................................................

..................................................................................................................................

..................................................................................................................................

..................................................................................................................................

..................................................................................................................................

**Centrioles -**

..................................................................................................................................

..................................................................................................................................

..................................................................................................................................

..................................................................................................................................

..................................................................................................................................

..................................................................................................................................

..................................................................................................................................

5. What is the difference between a **chromosome**, **a gene** and **DNA**?

..................................................................................................................................

..................................................................................................................................

..................................................................................................................................

..................................................................................................................................

..................................................................................................................................

..................................................................................................................................

..................................................................................................................................

6. What is the chain of events for producing a plant hormone in a cell and that hormone leaving the cell?

..................................................................................................
..................................................................................................
..................................................................................................
..................................................................................................
..................................................................................................
..................................................................................................
..................................................................................................

7. What are the differences between **prokaryotes** and **eukaryotes**?

..................................................................................................
..................................................................................................
..................................................................................................
..................................................................................................
..................................................................................................

8. Why are some **prokaryotes** important?

..................................................................................................
..................................................................................................
..................................................................................................
..................................................................................................
..................................................................................................

9. In what type of organism are most membrane bound organelles found?

..................................................................................................

10. What do the terms **hydrophobic** and **hydrophilic** mean?

   ...........................................................................................................................

   ...........................................................................................................................

   ...........................................................................................................................

   ...........................................................................................................................

   ...........................................................................................................................

   ...........................................................................................................................

11. What are membranes for?

   ...........................................................................................................................

   ...........................................................................................................................

   ...........................................................................................................................

   ...........................................................................................................................

   ...........................................................................................................................

   ...........................................................................................................................

   ...........................................................................................................................

   ...........................................................................................................................

12. What is a **phospholipid**?

   ...........................................................................................................................

   ...........................................................................................................................

   ...........................................................................................................................

13. What is a **phospholipid bilayer**?

   ...........................................................................................................................

   ...........................................................................................................................

   ...........................................................................................................................

   ...........................................................................................................................

14. What is the difference between molecules with charges and molecules without charges?

15. How do **bilayers** form?

16. Describe some different membrane structures.

# Membranes & Transport

The OCR specification states the following learning outcomes for membranes & transport:

**Candidates should be able to:**

(1) **State** that plasma (cell surface) membranes are partially permeable barriers;

(2) **Describe**, with the aid of diagrams, the fluid mosaic model of membrane structure (HSW1);

(3) **Describe** the roles of the components of the cell membrane; phospholipids, cholesterol, glycolipids, proteins and glycoproteins;

(4) **Outline** the effect of changing temperature on membrane structure and permeability;

(5) **Explain** the term cell signaling;

(6) **Explain** the role of membrane-bound receptors as sites where hormones and drugs can bind;

(7) **Explain** what is meant by passive transport (diffusion and facilitated diffusion including the role of membrane proteins), active transport, endocytosis and exocytosis;

# Membranes & Transport

1. What is meant by a **partially permeable membrane**?

   ..................................................................................................
   ..................................................................................................
   ..................................................................................................
   ..................................................................................................

2. What is the **Fluid Mosaic Model**?

   ..................................................................................................
   ..................................................................................................
   ..................................................................................................

3. What are the main features of the **Fluid Mosaic Model**?

   ..................................................................................................
   ..................................................................................................
   ..................................................................................................
   ..................................................................................................

4. What is a **glycolipid**?

   ..................................................................................................
   ..................................................................................................
   ..................................................................................................
   ..................................................................................................

5. What is a **glycoprotein**?

   ..................................................................................................
   ..................................................................................................
   ..................................................................................................
   ..................................................................................................

**BASIC QUESTIONS**

6. What do the following do in membranes:

**Cholesterol -**

..................................................................................................................
..................................................................................................................
..................................................................................................................
..................................................................................................................
..................................................................................................................

**Channel proteins -**

..................................................................................................................
..................................................................................................................
..................................................................................................................
..................................................................................................................
..................................................................................................................

**Carrier proteins -**

..................................................................................................................
..................................................................................................................
..................................................................................................................
..................................................................................................................
..................................................................................................................

**Receptor sites -**

..................................................................................................................
..................................................................................................................
..................................................................................................................
..................................................................................................................
..................................................................................................................

**Enzymes and Coenzymes -**

..................................................................................................
..................................................................................................
..................................................................................................
..................................................................................................
..................................................................................................

7. What happens when you increase the temperature of a membrane?

..................................................................................................
..................................................................................................
..................................................................................................

8. What is **cell signalling**?

..................................................................................................
..................................................................................................
..................................................................................................

9. How does the **insulin receptor** work?

..................................................................................................
..................................................................................................
..................................................................................................
..................................................................................................
..................................................................................................

10. How do medicines interfere with receptors?

..................................................................................................
..................................................................................................
..................................................................................................
..................................................................................................

11. What effect can **viruses** have on receptors?

   ................................................................................................................
   ................................................................................................................
   ................................................................................................................
   ................................................................................................................

12. What is **kinetic energy**?

   ................................................................................................................
   ................................................................................................................

13. What are the passive processes for crossing cell membranes. Describe how they work.

   ................................................................................................................
   ................................................................................................................
   ................................................................................................................
   ................................................................................................................
   ................................................................................................................
   ................................................................................................................
   ................................................................................................................
   ................................................................................................................
   ................................................................................................................
   ................................................................................................................
   ................................................................................................................
   ................................................................................................................
   ................................................................................................................

14. Give some examples of **diffusion** and **facilitated diffusion**.

...................................................................................................................................
...................................................................................................................................
...................................................................................................................................
...................................................................................................................................
...................................................................................................................................
...................................................................................................................................
...................................................................................................................................
...................................................................................................................................
...................................................................................................................................
...................................................................................................................................

15. How can the rate of the passive processes be effected?

...................................................................................................................................
...................................................................................................................................
...................................................................................................................................
...................................................................................................................................
...................................................................................................................................
...................................................................................................................................
...................................................................................................................................

16. How are the types of molecules allowed into a cell controlled?

...................................................................................................................................
...................................................................................................................................
...................................................................................................................................
...................................................................................................................................
...................................................................................................................................

17. What is **active transport**?

...................................................................................................................................
...................................................................................................................................
...................................................................................................................................

18. How are large amounts of liquid and solids moved into and out of cells?

   ......................................................................................................................

   ......................................................................................................................

   ......................................................................................................................

19. Give an example of **active transport**.

   ......................................................................................................................

   ......................................................................................................................

   ......................................................................................................................

   ......................................................................................................................

   ......................................................................................................................

# Water

The OCR specification states the following learning outcomes for water:

**Candidates should be able to:**

(1) **Explain** what is meant by osmosis, in terms of water potential. (No calculations of water potential will be required);

(2) **Recognise and explain** the effects that solutions of different water potentials can have upon plant and animal cells (HSW3)

BASIC QUESTIONS

# Water

1. What is **osmosis**?

   ...................................................................................................
   ...................................................................................................
   ...................................................................................................

2. What do the following mean?

   **Solute -**

   ...................................................................................................
   ...................................................................................................

   **Solvent -**

   ...................................................................................................
   ...................................................................................................

   **Solution -**

   ...................................................................................................
   ...................................................................................................

3. What is **'free' water**?

   ...................................................................................................
   ...................................................................................................
   ...................................................................................................

4. What is a **water potential**?

   ...................................................................................................
   ...................................................................................................
   ...................................................................................................

5. What is **water potential** measured in and what is the highest water potential?

   ...............................................................................................................

   ...............................................................................................................

   ...............................................................................................................

6. How do cells become **turgid** or **haemolysed**?

   ...............................................................................................................

   ...............................................................................................................

   ...............................................................................................................

   ...............................................................................................................

   ...............................................................................................................

   ...............................................................................................................

   ...............................................................................................................

7. How do cells become **plasmolysed** or **crenated**?

   ...............................................................................................................

   ...............................................................................................................

   ...............................................................................................................

   ...............................................................................................................

   ...............................................................................................................

   ...............................................................................................................

8. What happens to cells in solutions of:

   **High water potential -**

   ...............................................................................................................

   ...............................................................................................................

   ...............................................................................................................

   ...............................................................................................................

   ...............................................................................................................

**Low water potential -**

# Cell Cycles & Divisions

The OCR specification states the following learning outcomes for cell cycles & divisions:

**BASIC QUESTIONS**

Candidates should be able to:

(1) **State** that mitosis occupies only a small percentage of the cell cycle and that the remaining percentage includes the copying and checking of genetic information;

(2) **Describe**, with the aid of diagrams and photographs, the main stages of mitosis (behaviour of the chromosomes, nuclear envelope, cell membrane and centrioles);

(3) **Explain** the meaning of the term homologous pair of chromosomes;

(4) **Explain** the significance of mitosis for growth, repair and asexual reproduction in plants and animals;

(5) **Outline**, with the aid of diagrams and photographs, the process of cell division by budding in yeast;

(6) **State** that cells produced as a result of meiosis are not genetically identical (details of meiosis are not required);

(7) **Define** the term stem cell;

(8) **Define** the term differentiation, with reference to the production of erythrocytes (red blood cells) and neutrophils derived from stem cells in bone marrow, and the production of xylem vessels and phloem sieve tubes from cambium;

(9) **Describe and explain**, with the aid of diagrams and photographs, how cells of multicellular organisms are specialised for particular functions, with reference to erythrocytes (red blood cells), neutrophils, epithelial cells, sperm cells, palisade cells, root hair cells and guard cells;

# Cell Cycles & Divisions

1. What happens in the **cell cycle**? Explain each phase.

2. What are the products of the **cell cycle**?

3. What is **chromatin**?

4. How are **mutations** detected?

5. What is the speed of the **cell cycle**?

6. Apart from **chromosomes**, what else do **daughter cells** need?

7. What is **mitosis**?

8. What happens in each of the following phases:

   **Prophase -**

**Metaphase -**

..................................................

**Anaphase -**

..................................................

**Telophase -**

..................................................

9. Do **bacteria** conduct **mitosis**?

..................................................

10. Where does **mitosis** occur in plants? What cells can conduct **mitosis** in plants?

..................................................................................................
..................................................................................................
..................................................................................................
..................................................................................................

11. What is a **clone**?

..................................................................................................
..................................................................................................

12. What is **binary fission**?

..................................................................................................
..................................................................................................
..................................................................................................
..................................................................................................
..................................................................................................

13. What is a **stem cell**, how is it different to a normal cell?

..................................................................................................
..................................................................................................
..................................................................................................
..................................................................................................
..................................................................................................

BASIC QUESTIONS

14. Describe the steps for cloning animals.

...................................................................................................................................

...................................................................................................................................

...................................................................................................................................

...................................................................................................................................

...................................................................................................................................

...................................................................................................................................

...................................................................................................................................

...................................................................................................................................

...................................................................................................................................

15. What is **cytokinesis**?

...................................................................................................................................

...................................................................................................................................

16. How are genetically different cells produced?

...................................................................................................................................

...................................................................................................................................

17. What are the differences between **mitosis** and **meiosis**?

...................................................................................................................................

...................................................................................................................................

...................................................................................................................................

...................................................................................................................................

...................................................................................................................................

...................................................................................................................................

...................................................................................................................................

18. What is **differentiation**?

......................................................................................................................................

......................................................................................................................................

......................................................................................................................................

19. Is energy made in a cell?

......................................................................................................................................

......................................................................................................................................

......................................................................................................................................

20. How can cells **differentiate**?

......................................................................................................................................

......................................................................................................................................

......................................................................................................................................

21. What is special about **erythrocytes** and **neutrophils**?

......................................................................................................................................

......................................................................................................................................

......................................................................................................................................

......................................................................................................................................

22. What role do **lysosomes** play in **neutrophils**?

......................................................................................................................................

......................................................................................................................................

......................................................................................................................................

......................................................................................................................................

......................................................................................................................................

# Organism Organisation

The OCR specification states the following learning outcomes for organism organisation:

### Candidates should be able to:

(1) **Explain** the meaning of the terms tissue, organ and organ system;

(2) **Explain**, with the aid of diagrams and photographs, how cells are organised into tissues, using squamous and ciliated epithelia, xylem and phloem as examples;

(3) **Discuss** the importance of cooperation between cells, tissues, organs and organ systems (HSW4)

# Organism Organisation

**BASIC QUESTIONS**

1. Give definitions of the following:

   **Tissues -**
   ...................................................................................................................................
   ...................................................................................................................................
   ...................................................................................................................................

   **Organs -**
   ...................................................................................................................................
   ...................................................................................................................................
   ...................................................................................................................................

   **Organ systems -**
   ...................................................................................................................................
   ...................................................................................................................................
   ...................................................................................................................................

2. What are the different roles of **xylem** and phloem in plants?
   ...................................................................................................................................
   ...................................................................................................................................
   ...................................................................................................................................
   ...................................................................................................................................

3. What is **squamous epithelial tissue**?
   ...................................................................................................................................
   ...................................................................................................................................

4. What is **ciliated epithelial tissue**?

　　...................................................................................................................
　　...................................................................................................................
　　...................................................................................................................

5. How have leaves adapted to their function?

　　...................................................................................................................
　　...................................................................................................................
　　...................................................................................................................
　　...................................................................................................................
　　...................................................................................................................

6. What is special about **stomata**?

　　...................................................................................................................
　　...................................................................................................................
　　...................................................................................................................

7. How are **muscles** and the **nervous system** connected?

　　...................................................................................................................
　　...................................................................................................................
　　...................................................................................................................

# Exchange & the Lungs

The OCR specification states the following learning outcomes for Exchange & The Lungs:

Candidates should be able to:

(1) **Explain**, in terms of surface area:volume ratio, why multicellular organisms need specialised exchange surfaces and single-celled organisms do not (HSW1);

(2) **Describe** the features of an efficient exchange surface, with reference to diffusion of oxygen and carbon dioxide across an alveolus;

(3) **Describe** the features of the mammalian lung that adapt it to efficient gaseous exchange;

(4) **Describe**, with the aid of diagrams and photographs, the distribution of cartilage, ciliated epithelium, goblet cells, smooth muscle and elastic fibres in the trachea, bronchi, bronchioles and alveoli of the mammalian gaseous exchange system;

(5) **Describe** the functions of cartilage, cilia, goblet cells, smooth muscle and elastic fibres in the mammalian gaseous exchange system;

(6) **Outline** the mechanism of breathing (inspiration and expiration) in mammals, with reference to the function of the rib cage, intercostal muscles and diaphragm;

(7) **Explain** the meanings of the terms tidal volume and vital capacity;

(8) **Describe** how a spirometer can be used to measure vital capacity, tidal volume, breathing rate and oxygen uptake;

(9) **Analyse** and interpret data from a spirometer.

BASIC QUESTIONS

# Exchange & the Lungs

1. What is an **exchange surface**?

   ..................................................................................................

   ..................................................................................................

2. Why are **exchange surfaces** needed?

   ..................................................................................................

   ..................................................................................................

   ..................................................................................................

   ..................................................................................................

3. Give some examples of different **exchange surfaces**. What attributes must they have?

   ..................................................................................................

   ..................................................................................................

   ..................................................................................................

   ..................................................................................................

   ..................................................................................................

4. Describe the structure of the human lungs.

   ..................................................................................................

   ..................................................................................................

   ..................................................................................................

   ..................................................................................................

   ..................................................................................................

   ..................................................................................................

   ..................................................................................................

5. How is effective gaseous exchange facilitated in the human respiratory system?

..................................................................................................................

..................................................................................................................

..................................................................................................................

..................................................................................................................

6. Describe the processes of:

**Inspiration -**

..................................................................................................................

..................................................................................................................

..................................................................................................................

..................................................................................................................

..................................................................................................................

..................................................................................................................

..................................................................................................................

..................................................................................................................

..................................................................................................................

**Expiration -**

..................................................................................................................

..................................................................................................................

..................................................................................................................

..................................................................................................................

..................................................................................................................

..................................................................................................................

..................................................................................................................

7. What similarities and differences do the **trachea** and **bronchi** have?

..................................................................................................................................

..................................................................................................................................

..................................................................................................................................

..................................................................................................................................

8. Complete the following table:

| Tissue | Role |
|---|---|
| Smooth Muscle | |
| Elastic Fibres | |
| Goblet Cells & Glandular Tissue | |
| Ciliated Epithelium | |

9. What role do the **diaphragm** and **intercostal muscles** have?

..................................................................................................................

..................................................................................................................

..................................................................................................................

..................................................................................................................

..................................................................................................................

..................................................................................................................

10. What is the difference between **breathing** and **respiration**?

..................................................................................................................

..................................................................................................................

..................................................................................................................

11. Describe the different elements of lung volume.

..................................................................................................................

..................................................................................................................

..................................................................................................................

..................................................................................................................

..................................................................................................................

..................................................................................................................

..................................................................................................................

..................................................................................................................

12. How can a **spirometer** be used to measure lung capacity?

..................................................................................................................

..................................................................................................................

..................................................................................................................

..................................................................................................................

..................................................................................................................

# Transport in Animals

The OCR specification states the following learning outcomes for Transport in Animals:

### Candidates should be able to:

(1) **Explain** the need for transport systems in multicellular animals in terms of size, level of activity and surface area:volume ratio;

(2) **Explain** the meaning of the terms single circulatory system and double circulatory system, with reference to the circulatory systems of fish and mammals;

(3) **Explain** the meaning of the terms open circulatory system and closed circulatory system, with reference to the circulatory systems of insects and fish;

(4) **Describe**, with the aid of diagrams and photographs, the external and internal structure of the mammalian heart;

(5) **Explain**, with the aid of diagrams, the differences in the thickness of the walls of the different chambers of the heart in terms of their functions;

(6) **Describe** the cardiac cycle, with reference to the action of the valves in the heart;

(7) **Describe** how heart action is coordinated with reference to the sinoatrial node (SAN), the atrioventricular node (AVN) and the Purkyne tissue;

(8) **interpret** and explain electrocardiogram (ECG) traces, with reference to normal and abnormal heart activity;

(9) **Describe**, with the aid of diagrams and photographs, the structures and functions of arteries, veins and capillaries;

(10) **Explain** the differences between blood, tissue fluid and lymph;

(11) **Describe** how tissue fluid is formed from plasma;

(12) **Describe** the role of haemoglobin in carrying oxygen and carbon dioxide;

(13) **Describe** and explain the significance of the dissociation curves of adult oxyhaemoglobin at different carbon dioxide levels (the Bohr effect);

(14) **Explain** the significance of the different affinities of fetal haemoglobin and adult haemoglobin for oxygen

# Transport in Animals

**BASIC QUESTIONS**

1. What is the significance of **surface area** to **volume ratio**?

   ...........................................................................................................................
   ...........................................................................................................................
   ...........................................................................................................................

2. Describe the differences and advantages and disadvantages of single and double circulatory systems.

   ...........................................................................................................................
   ...........................................................................................................................
   ...........................................................................................................................
   ...........................................................................................................................
   ...........................................................................................................................
   ...........................................................................................................................
   ...........................................................................................................................
   ...........................................................................................................................
   ...........................................................................................................................
   ...........................................................................................................................

3. Describe the route taken by blood as it enters and then leaves the **heart**. Include it's oxygen state and if nervous impulses are used.

....................................................................................................

4. How does **blood pressure** change as blood moves through the **heart**?

....................................................................................................

5. Complete the following diagram of the heart by labelling each part.

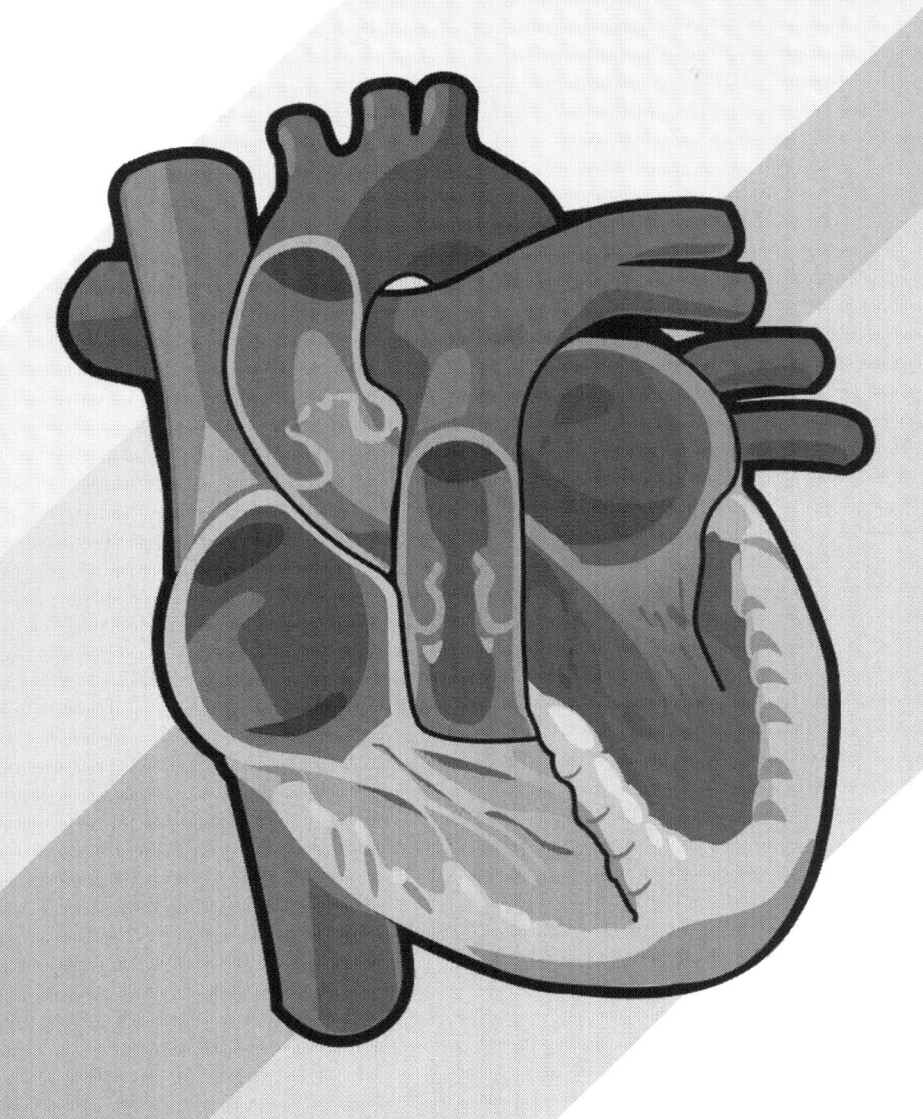

BASIC QUESTIONS

6. What occurs in **atrial contraction**?

..................................................................................................................................
..................................................................................................................................
..................................................................................................................................
..................................................................................................................................
..................................................................................................................................

7. What occurs in **ventricular contraction**?

　

8. What is the difference between **diastole** and **systole**?

　

9. What do the **atrioventricular valves** do?

　

10. What do the **semilunar valves** do?

11. What causes the sounds of the heart beat?

12. How is the heart beat initiated?

13. How is contraction of the **atria** achieved?

14. How is contraction of the **ventricles** achieved?

BASIC QUESTIONS

15. What does an **electrocardiogram** show?

   ............................................................................................................
   ............................................................................................................
   ............................................................................................................
   ............................................................................................................

16. What is the difference between an open and a closed circulatory system?

   ............................................................................................................
   ............................................................................................................
   ............................................................................................................
   ............................................................................................................
   ............................................................................................................
   ............................................................................................................
   ............................................................................................................
   ............................................................................................................

17. What is **tissue fluid**?

   ............................................................................................................
   ............................................................................................................
   ............................................................................................................
   ............................................................................................................

18. What is the **endothelium** of a blood vessel?

   ............................................................................................................
   ............................................................................................................
   ............................................................................................................
   ............................................................................................................

19. Complete the table about the attributes of **arteries**.

| Attribute | Structure / Function |
|---|---|
| Lumen | |
| Wall | |
| Elastic tissue | |
| Smooth muscle | |
| Endothelium | |

20. Complete the table about the attributes of **veins**.

| Attribute | Structure / Function |
|---|---|
| Lumen | |
| Wall | |
| Valves | |

21. Complete the table about the attributes of **capillaries**.

| Attribute | Structure / Function |
|---|---|
| Lumen | |
| Wall | |

22. What are **platelets** and what do they do?

..................................................................................
..................................................................................
..................................................................................
..................................................................................
..................................................................................

23. What is **hydrostatic pressure**?

..................................................................................
..................................................................................
..................................................................................

24. Describe how **tissue fluid** is formed.

..................................................................................
..................................................................................
..................................................................................
..................................................................................
..................................................................................
..................................................................................
..................................................................................
..................................................................................
..................................................................................
..................................................................................
..................................................................................
..................................................................................
..................................................................................
..................................................................................
..................................................................................

25. What is a **lymphocyte**?

   ........................................................................................
   ........................................................................................
   ........................................................................................

26. How is **lymph** formed?

   ........................................................................................
   ........................................................................................
   ........................................................................................
   ........................................................................................
   ........................................................................................
   ........................................................................................

27. What is **haemoglobin**?

   ........................................................................................
   ........................................................................................
   ........................................................................................

28. What does it mean when something has an **affinity** for something?

   ........................................................................................
   ........................................................................................
   ........................................................................................

29. What is **dissociation**?

   ........................................................................................
   ........................................................................................
   ........................................................................................

30. What is **partial pressure / oxygen tension**?

...................................................................................................................................
...................................................................................................................................
...................................................................................................................................
...................................................................................................................................
...................................................................................................................................
...................................................................................................................................

31. What does an **oxygen dissociation curve** show?

...................................................................................................................................
...................................................................................................................................
...................................................................................................................................
...................................................................................................................................
...................................................................................................................................
...................................................................................................................................
...................................................................................................................................
...................................................................................................................................
...................................................................................................................................
...................................................................................................................................
...................................................................................................................................

32. How does **foetal haemoglobin** differ from **adult haemoglobin**?

...................................................................................................................................
...................................................................................................................................
...................................................................................................................................
...................................................................................................................................
...................................................................................................................................
...................................................................................................................................

33. What is **carbaminohaemoglobin**?

34. How is carbon dioxide transported in the body?

35. Describe the **chloride shift**.

36. How is oxygen released to the tissues of the body?

37. Describe the **Bohr effect**.

# Transport in Plants

The OCR specification states the following learning outcomes for Transport in Plants:

### Candidates should be able to:

(1) **Explain** the need for transport systems in multicellular plants in terms of size and surface area:volume ratio;

(2) **Describe**, with the aid of diagrams and photographs, the distribution of xylem and phloem tissue in roots, stems and leaves of dicotyledonous plants;

(3) **Describe**, with the aid of diagrams and photographs, the structure and function of xylem vessels, sieve tube elements and companion cells;

(4) **Define** the term transpiration;

(5) **Explain** why transpiration is a consequence of gaseous exchange;

(6) **Describe** the factors that affect transpiration rate;

(7) **Describe**, with the aid of diagrams, how a potometer is used to estimate transpiration rates (HSW3);

(8) **Explain**, in terms of water potential, the movement of water between plant cells, and between plant cells and their environment. (No calculations involving water potential will be set);

(9) **Describe**, with the aid of diagrams, the pathway by which water is transported from the root cortex to the air surrounding the leaves, with reference to the Casparian strip, apoplast pathway, symplast pathway, xylem and the stomata;

(10) **Explain** the mechanism by which water is transported from the root cortex to the air surrounding the leaves, with reference to adhesion, cohesion and the transpiration stream;

(11) **Describe**, with the aid of diagrams and photographs, how the leaves of some xerophytes are adapted to reduce water loss by transpiration;

(12) **Explain** translocation as an energy-requiring process transporting assimilates, especially sucrose, between sources (eg leaves) and sinks (eg roots, meristem);

(13) **Describe**, with the aid of diagrams, the mechanism of transport in phloem involving active loading at the source and removal at the sink, and the evidence for and against this mechanism (HSW1, 7a).

# Transport in Plants

**BASIC QUESTIONS**

1. What is **vascular tissue**?

   ..................................................................................................................................
   ..................................................................................................................................
   ..................................................................................................................................

2. What do the **xylem** vessels do?

   ..................................................................................................................................
   ..................................................................................................................................
   ..................................................................................................................................

3. What do the **phloem** vessels do?

   ..................................................................................................................................
   ..................................................................................................................................
   ..................................................................................................................................

4. What are **vascular** bundles?

   ..................................................................................................................................
   ..................................................................................................................................
   ..................................................................................................................................

5. What is the role of the **endodermis**?

   ..................................................................................................................................
   ..................................................................................................................................
   ..................................................................................................................................

6. What are **meristem** cells?

   ..................................................................................................................................
   ..................................................................................................................................
   ..................................................................................................................................

7. What is the **pericycle**?

   ......................................................................................................
   ......................................................................................................
   ......................................................................................................

8. Describe the position of the **xylem** and phloem **vessels** within a plant.

   ......................................................................................................
   ......................................................................................................
   ......................................................................................................
   ......................................................................................................
   ......................................................................................................
   ......................................................................................................
   ......................................................................................................
   ......................................................................................................
   ......................................................................................................
   ......................................................................................................
   ......................................................................................................
   ......................................................................................................

9. Describe the structure of a **xylem** vessel.

...................................................................................................................................

...................................................................................................................................

...................................................................................................................................

...................................................................................................................................

...................................................................................................................................

...................................................................................................................................

...................................................................................................................................

...................................................................................................................................

...................................................................................................................................

...................................................................................................................................

...................................................................................................................................

...................................................................................................................................

10. What are the adaptations of **xylem** for its function?

...................................................................................................................................

...................................................................................................................................

...................................................................................................................................

...................................................................................................................................

...................................................................................................................................

...................................................................................................................................

...................................................................................................................................

...................................................................................................................................

...................................................................................................................................

...................................................................................................................................

...................................................................................................................................

...................................................................................................................................

BASIC QUESTIONS

11. Describe the structure of a **phloem** vessel.

...........................................................................................................................
...........................................................................................................................
...........................................................................................................................
...........................................................................................................................
...........................................................................................................................
...........................................................................................................................
...........................................................................................................................
...........................................................................................................................
...........................................................................................................................
...........................................................................................................................
...........................................................................................................................
...........................................................................................................................
...........................................................................................................................

12. What is the role of the **sieve tubes**?

...........................................................................................................................
...........................................................................................................................
...........................................................................................................................
...........................................................................................................................
...........................................................................................................................

13. What is the role of the **companion cells**?

...........................................................................................................................
...........................................................................................................................
...........................................................................................................................
...........................................................................................................................
...........................................................................................................................

14. What is **water potential**?

...................................................................................................

...................................................................................................

...................................................................................................

...................................................................................................

15. What is a **turgid** cell?

...................................................................................................

...................................................................................................

...................................................................................................

...................................................................................................

16. What is **plasmolysis**?

...................................................................................................

...................................................................................................

...................................................................................................

...................................................................................................

17. What are the mains points about **water potential**?

...................................................................................................

...................................................................................................

...................................................................................................

...................................................................................................

...................................................................................................

...................................................................................................

...................................................................................................

18. Complete the table about movement of water between plant cells.

| Pathway | Description |
|---|---|
| Apoplast | |
| Symplast | |
| Vacuolar | |

19. What do the **root hair cells** do?

..................................................................................................................................
..................................................................................................................................
..................................................................................................................................
..................................................................................................................................
..................................................................................................................................

20. How does water move across the root?

..................................................................................................................................
..................................................................................................................................
..................................................................................................................................
..................................................................................................................................

21. What does the **Casparian strip** do?

........................................................................................

........................................................................................

........................................................................................

........................................................................................

........................................................................................

........................................................................................

........................................................................................

........................................................................................

........................................................................................

........................................................................................

22. How does **root pressure** aid water to move up the stem?

........................................................................................

........................................................................................

........................................................................................

........................................................................................

........................................................................................

23. What is **transpiration pull**?

........................................................................................

........................................................................................

24. What is the **cohesion-tension theory**?

........................................................................................

........................................................................................

........................................................................................

........................................................................................

........................................................................................

25. How does **capillary action** aid water movement?

...........................................................................................................................

...........................................................................................................................

...........................................................................................................................

...........................................................................................................................

...........................................................................................................................

26. How does water leave the leaf?

...........................................................................................................................

...........................................................................................................................

...........................................................................................................................

...........................................................................................................................

...........................................................................................................................

27. What is **transpiration**?

...........................................................................................................................

...........................................................................................................................

...........................................................................................................................

...........................................................................................................................

...........................................................................................................................

28. What is **water vapour potential**?

...........................................................................................................................

...........................................................................................................................

...........................................................................................................................

...........................................................................................................................

...........................................................................................................................

29. Why is water movement within a plant useful?

30. When a plant loses too much water, what happens to it?

31. Complete the table on the factors effecting water loss.

| Affecting Factor | Consequence |
|---|---|
| Air movement | |
| Temperature | |
| Number of leaves | |
| Amount of light | |
| Stomata | |

| Affecting Factor | Consequence |
|---|---|
| Availability of water | |
| Cuticle | |
| Humidity | |

BASIC QUESTIONS

32. What is a **xerophyte**?

..................................................................................................................................
..................................................................................................................................
..................................................................................................................................

33. How do **xerophytes** prevent water loss?

..........................................................................................................................
..........................................................................................................................
..........................................................................................................................
..........................................................................................................................
..........................................................................................................................
..........................................................................................................................
..........................................................................................................................
..........................................................................................................................
..........................................................................................................................
..........................................................................................................................
..........................................................................................................................
..........................................................................................................................
..........................................................................................................................
..........................................................................................................................

34. What is **translocation**?

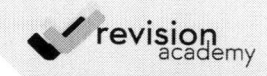

..........................................................................................................................
..........................................................................................................................
..........................................................................................................................
..........................................................................................................................

35. Describe how sucrose enters the **phloem**.

..................................................................................................

..................................................................................................

..................................................................................................

..................................................................................................

..................................................................................................

..................................................................................................

..................................................................................................

..................................................................................................

..................................................................................................

..................................................................................................

..................................................................................................

36. What is the difference between a **source** and a **sink** of sucrose?

..................................................................................................

..................................................................................................

..................................................................................................

..................................................................................................

..................................................................................................

..................................................................................................

37. What is **mass flow**?

..................................................................................................

..................................................................................................

..................................................................................................

..................................................................................................

..................................................................................................

# Smart Notes

In this section all of the most difficult parts of the exam are considered and space is made available for you to record the most important information.

This can be done in note form, bullet points or diagrams. It is a useful way of keeping all your notes in one place so you may refer back to them easily if you need to.

# Organelles

# Transport across membranes

# Cell Signalling

# Osmosis

SMART NOTES

# Mitosis

# Lungs

SMART NOTES

# Cardiac Cycle

# Bohr Shift

# Chloride Shift

# Tissue Fluid

**SMART NOTES**

# Transpiration

# Translocation

SMART NOTES

# Past Paper Contents

In this section we have reviewed all the available past papers for this particular exam and highlighted the topic of each question within each paper.

This will help you to quickly identify the past paper you wish to use to test particular knowledge of a specific subject.

The past papers can be accessed from the Exam boards website. Alternatively you may register with us and download them from our website www.therevisionacademy.co.uk.

# Past Paper Contents

| Date | Question | Content |
|---|---|---|
| **Jan 2009** | 1 | Labelling animal cell, organelles, production of proteins, calculation question |
| | 2 | Plasmolysed and turgid cells, water potential, transport across membranes |
| | 3 | Stem cells, mitosis |
| | 4 | Surface area, gas exchange systems, inspiration |
| | 5 | Heart, action of heart |
| | 6 | Translocation |
| **June 2009** | 1 | Structure of the lung, lung cell function |
| | 2 | Fluid mosaic model, cell signalling, How Science Works question (HSW) |
| | 3 | Water loss from plants |
| | 4 | Prokaryotic & Eukaryotic cells |
| | 5 | Cell cycle, meiosis |
| | 6 | Heart, calculation question |
| **Jan 2010** | 1 | Microscopy, xylem |
| | 2 | Tissues in the lung, |
| | 3 | Transport through membranes, glycoproteins |
| | 4 | Potometer, HSW, calculation question |
| | 5 | Blood vessels, hydrostatic pressure, tissue fluid, chloride shift |
| | 6 | Spirometer, inspiration, vital capacity |
| **May 2010** | 1 | Bacterium structure, eukaryotic & prokaryotic cells, functions of cells and tissues |
| | 2 | Microscopy, foetal haemoglobin, Bohr shift |
| | 3 | Active transport, HSW, budding in yeast |
| | 4 | Plant & animal cell differences, cell adaptations, meiosis |
| | 5 | Water pathways through plants, water movement through xylem, difference between xylem & phloem |
| | 6 | ECG calculation, SAN |

| Date | Question | Content |
| --- | --- | --- |
| Jan 2011 | 1 | Mitosis |
| | 2 | Alveoli, cell signalling |
| | 3 | Oxygen transport |
| | 4 | Xylem & phloem, transpiration, |
| | 5 | Eukaryotic cells, microscopy calculation, organelles, neutrophils |
| | 6 | Osmosis, water pathways, water potential, HSW |
| June 2011 | 1 | Organelles, organs, gas exchange |
| | 2 | cell surface membrane, active transport, transport across membranes |
| | 3 | Heart structure, heart valves |
| | 4 | Meristems, HSW calculation, meiosis |
| | 5 | Spirometer |
| | 6 | Translocation, Phloem |
| Jan 2012 | 1 | Alveoli, elastic fibres, gas exchange |
| | 2 | Cell specialisation, flagellum, xylem & phloem |
| | 3 | Blood, tissue fluid & lymph, arteris |
| | 4 | Microscopy, calculation, nuclear pores |
| | 5 | Potometer, transpiration, xerophytes |
| | 6 | Cell membranes, vesicles, enzyme secretion |
| June 2012 | 1 | Yeast, cell division, tissues, epithelium |
| | 2 | Organelles, glogi apparatus, prokaryotiv vs eukaryotic |
| | 3 | Single vs double circulatory systems, blood pressure |
| | 4 | Water uptake by cells, oxygen transport, root hair cells |
| | 5 | Gas exchange in the lung, calculation |
| | 6 | Translocation, HSW |

| Date | Question | Content |
|---|---|---|
| **Jan 2013** | 1 | Heart structure, heart excitation, purkyne tissue |
| | 2 | Asexual reproduction, calculation, organisation of cells in an organism |
| | 3 | Fluid mosaic model, cell signalling |
| | 4 | Potometer, HSW |
| | 5 | Organelles |
| | 6 | Xylem and lignin, cartilage in trachea, gas exchange |

# Linked Topic Questions

Increasingly we have seen exam papers include questions that require knowledge across all topics within the unit and also from previous units.

Therefore we have come up with questions that link topics together and require real in-depth knowledge of the subject content.

These questions will really test your knowledge and your ability to apply it together with other concepts.

Remember to think outside the box, these are not just questions on one particular topic!

## Linked Topic Questions

1. How does the structure of a plant cell relate to the structure of a plant as a whole?

2. How does **meiosis** help to maintain **biodiversity**?

3. How are microscopes useful to determining information about organisms?

4. How can the movement of water across cell membranes aid other transport processes?

5. How can measuring **lung capacity** give an indication of oxygen transport within an individual?

# Flow Diagrams

This section contains flow diagrams of the major processes within the exam.

These can be used to test your knowledge by covering up the flow diagram and trying to remember each step.

In addition, writing the flow diagram out as a paragraph, as you would in an exam question, can be a really useful revision technique.

This is a useful tool to cement your knowledge on some tricky processes.

## Mitosis

DNA and organelles duplicate in interphase.

↓

Prophase: Chromatin shortens and thickens to visable chromosomes (which are Chromatids attached by Centrameres) and the nuclear envelope begins to break down.

↓

Metaphase: Centrioles move to the poles of the cell and spindle fibres form. Chromosomes arrange themselves along the equator attached to microtubules.

↓

Anaphase: Spindle fibres begin to shorten and Chromosomes are pulled apart at their Centromeres.

↓

Telophase: Chromosomes are at opposite ends of cell and nuclear envelopes begin to reform.

↓

Cytokinesis: Division into two separate cells.

↓

Two diploid daughter cells formed.

# Preparation of specimens for the light microscope

**STAINING: Coloured dyes are added to the specimen**

↓

These bind to chemicals within the specimen

↓

This allows the specimen to be seen

**SECTIONING: The specimen is embedded in wax**

↓

Thin sections are cut without distorting the specimen

↓

This allows section through viewing of structures

# Calibration of the eyepiece graticule

A stage micrometer is placed on the microscope slide

↓

This is a small ruler that is 1mm long and divided into 100 equal sections

↓

Each section is 0.01mm (10µm)

↓

Using a x4 objective lens and x10 eyepiece (x40 magnification)

↓

40 epu (eyepiece units) = 1mm (1000µm)

↓

1 epu = 25 µm

# Hormone production sequence

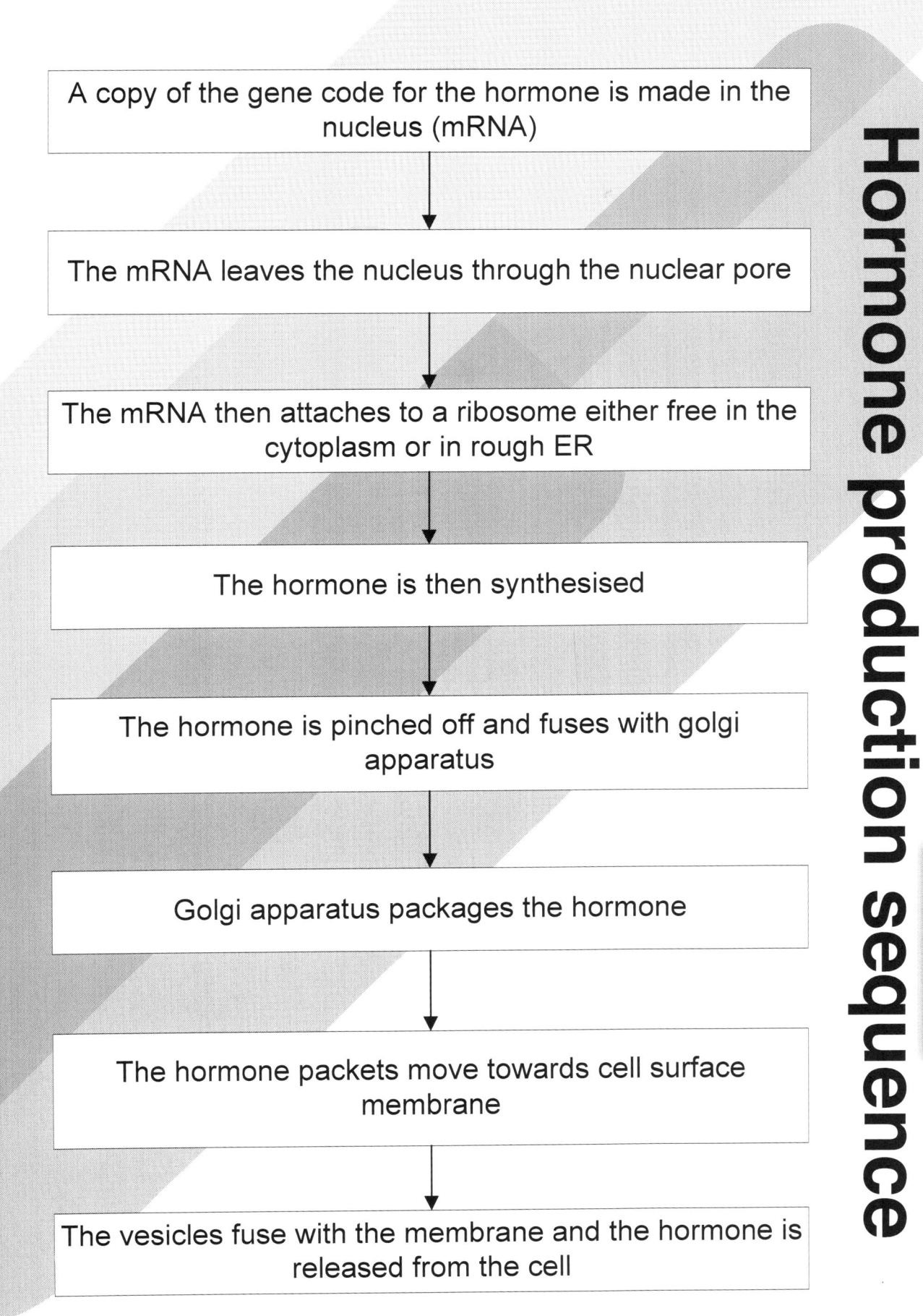

```
A copy of the gene code for the hormone is made in the nucleus (mRNA)
                            ↓
The mRNA leaves the nucleus through the nuclear pore
                            ↓
The mRNA then attaches to a ribosome either free in the cytoplasm or in rough ER
                            ↓
The hormone is then synthesised
                            ↓
The hormone is pinched off and fuses with golgi apparatus
                            ↓
Golgi apparatus packages the hormone
                            ↓
The hormone packets move towards cell surface membrane
                            ↓
The vesicles fuse with the membrane and the hormone is released from the cell
```

**FLOW DIAGRAMS**

# Active transport

```
Molecules are moving from an area of low
concentration to an area of high concentration
                    ↓
        Energy is required for this process
                    ↓
    The molecule combines with its specific carrier
                      protein
                    ↓
   A phosphate group from ATP is transferred to
   the carrier protein on the inside of the cell
                    membrane
                    ↓
      This changes the shape of the carrier protein
                    ↓
   The molecule is then carried across to the inside
                  of the membrane
                    ↓
   The molecule gets released into the inside and
   the carrier protein returns to its orginal shape
```

# Cloning

```
A tissue is taken from a donor animal
              ↓
These cells are then grown in a tissue culture
              ↓
The nucleus from a donor cell is transferred to an egg cell
              ↓
The embryo is now transferred to the uterus of a surrogate mother
              ↓
The foetus grows and is born
```

# Meiosis

DNA and organelles are duplicated during interphase.

↓

Prophase I: Chromatin shortens and thickens to visible chromosomes and the nuclear envelope breaks down. Homologous chromosomes pair up to form a bivalent.

↓

Bivalent cross each other, where they cross is known as Chiasma. This is called CROSSING OVER.

↓

Metaphase I: Spindle fibres form and bivalents line up at random on the equator. This is known as RANDOM ASSORTMENT.

↓

Anaphase I: Spindle fibres shorten and bivalents are pulled apart breaking off at the Chriasmata.

↓

Telephase I: Chromosomes are at the opposite ends of the cell and nuclear envelopes begin to reform.

↓

Prophase II to Cytokinesis is the same process without crossing over occuring

↓

Four haploid daughter cells are formed.

# Opening of stomata: Day

During photosynthesis in chloroplasts ATP is produced

↓

The ATP provides energy for the <u>active transport</u> of potassium ions into the guard cells

↓

This causes starch stored in the cells to convert to malate

↓

Malate is a soluble substance (starch is not) so the water potential of the cells are reduced

↓

Water moves into the cells via osmosis due to the water potential gradient

↓

This makes the guard cells turgid

↓

Once turgid the cells curve apart due to their outer walls being thinner than their inner walls

↓

Therefore the stomatal pore widens

**FLOW DIAGRAMS**

# Opening of Stomata: Night

> Photosynthesis does not occur at night in the chloroplasts

↓

> Therefore no ATP is produced here

↓

> With no ATP, potassium ions are __NOT__ actively transported and diffuse out of the guard cells

↓

> Therefore malate is converted back to insoluble starch

↓

> The water potential of the guard cells rises

↓

> Water moves out of the guard cells via osmosis down a water potential gradient

↓

> The guard cells become flacid

↓

> The stomatal pore closes

# Ventilation of the lungs: Inspiration

```
┌─────────────────────────────────────────────┐
│ Muscles contract in this process, therefore │
│ ATP is required                              │
└─────────────────────────────────────────────┘
                      ↓
┌─────────────────────────────────────────────┐
│ External intercostal muscles first contract │
└─────────────────────────────────────────────┘
                      ↓
┌─────────────────────────────────────────────┐
│ This pulls the ribs up and out              │
└─────────────────────────────────────────────┘
                      ↓
┌─────────────────────────────────────────────┐
│ As this occurs the muscles in the diaphragm │
│ contract and flatten                         │
└─────────────────────────────────────────────┘
                      ↓
┌─────────────────────────────────────────────┐
│ These processes increase the volume of the  │
│ thorax                                       │
└─────────────────────────────────────────────┘
                      ↓
┌─────────────────────────────────────────────┐
│ This increase in volume decreases pressure  │
│ within the lungs                             │
└─────────────────────────────────────────────┘
                      ↓
┌─────────────────────────────────────────────┐
│ Air is now drawn into the lungs as the      │
│ outside pressure is greater                  │
└─────────────────────────────────────────────┘
```

# Gas exchange in the Alveoli

Blood from the heart that is deoxygenated arrives from the lungs in capillaries

↓

These capillaries surround the alveolus

↓

Gaseous exchange is then able to occur from the air in the alveolus and the capillary

↓

Oxygen from the alveolus diffuses into capillaries

↓

Carbon dioxide from the deoxygenated blood diffuses out into the alevolus

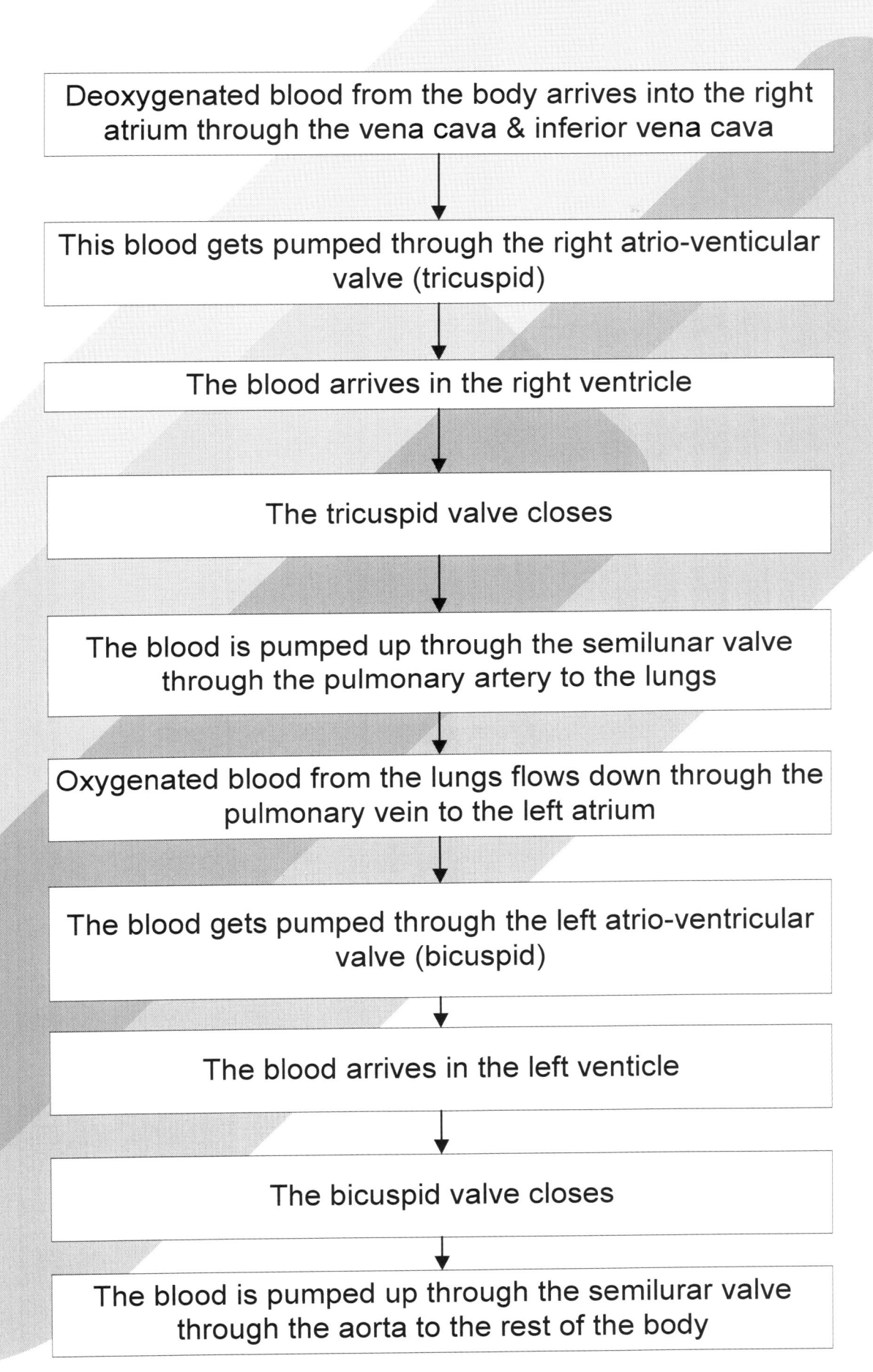

## Flow of blood through the heart

Deoxygenated blood from the body arrives into the right atrium through the vena cava & inferior vena cava

↓

This blood gets pumped through the right atrio-venticular valve (tricuspid)

↓

The blood arrives in the right ventricle

↓

The tricuspid valve closes

↓

The blood is pumped up through the semilunar valve through the pulmonary artery to the lungs

↓

Oxygenated blood from the lungs flows down through the pulmonary vein to the left atrium

↓

The blood gets pumped through the left atrio-ventricular valve (bicuspid)

↓

The blood arrives in the left venticle

↓

The bicuspid valve closes

↓

The blood is pumped up through the semilurar valve through the aorta to the rest of the body

# The Cell Cycle

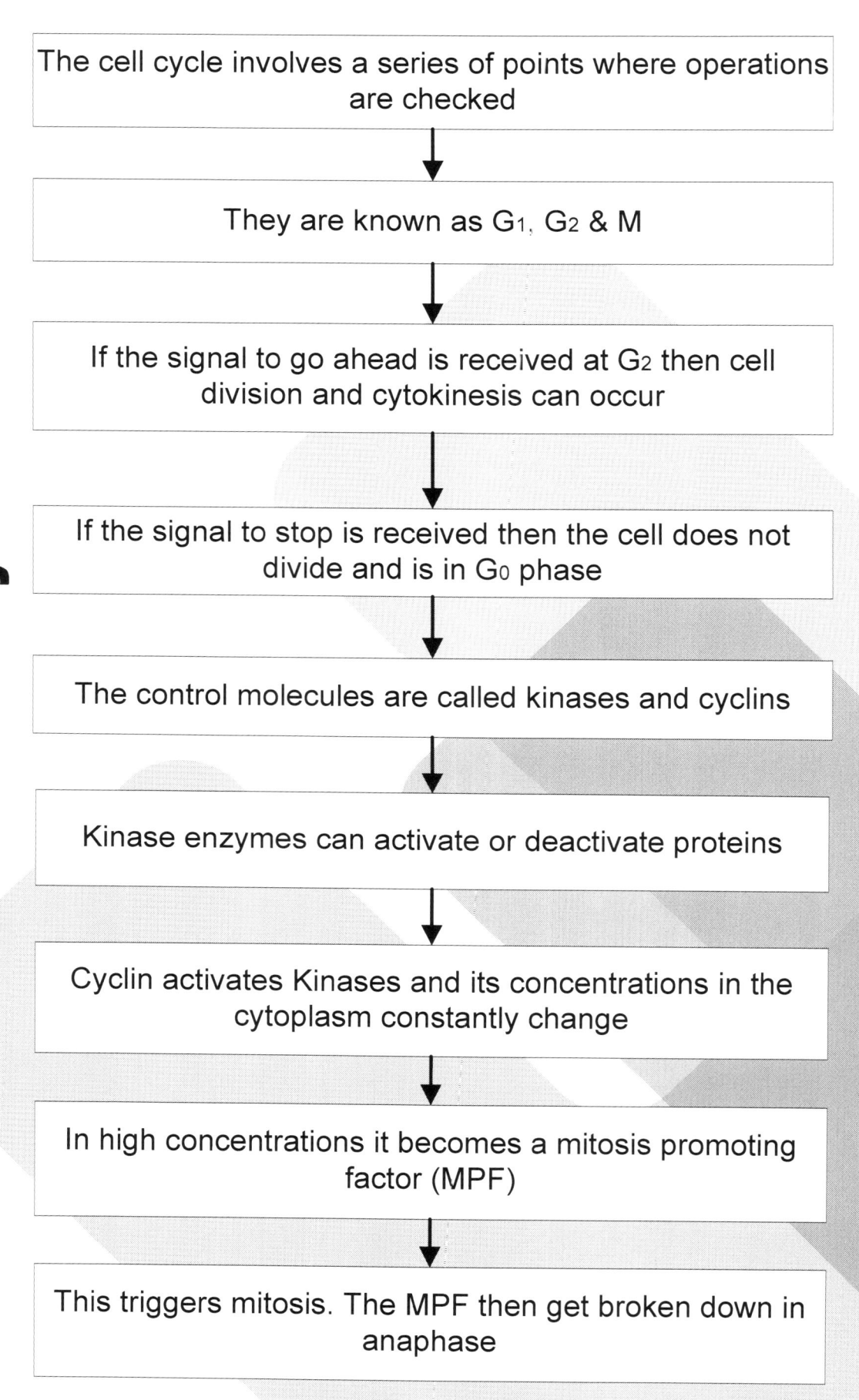

The cell cycle involves a series of points where operations are checked

↓

They are known as $G_1$, $G_2$ & M

↓

If the signal to go ahead is received at $G_2$ then cell division and cytokinesis can occur

↓

If the signal to stop is received then the cell does not divide and is in $G_0$ phase

↓

The control molecules are called kinases and cyclins

↓

Kinase enzymes can activate or deactivate proteins

↓

Cyclin activates Kinases and its concentrations in the cytoplasm constantly change

↓

In high concentrations it becomes a mitosis promoting factor (MPF)

↓

This triggers mitosis. The MPF then get broken down in anaphase

# Water Uptake by Plants

Water moves from the high water potential soil solution into the root hair cell down a water potential gradient by Osmosis.

↓

Water then moves through the three pathways,
Apoplast – through the cell wall.
Symplast – through Cytoplasm, Plasmodesmata.
Vacuolar – through the Vacuoles.

↓

At the Xylem the Casparian strip exists which prevents the use of the Apoplast pathway.

↓

Salts are actively transported into the Xylem to reduce the water potential within it.

↓

Water moves into the Xylem by Osmosis, this created root pressure.

**FLOW DIAGRAMS**

# Formation of Tissue Fluid

As blood moves into the capillary hydrostatic pressure increases

↓

This increase in hydrostatic pressure forces the fluid in the blood through the capillary walls

↓

The water potential within the blood is actually lower than that surrounding the cells

↓

However the hydrostatic pressure is greater, hence a net movement out of the capillary

↓

Solutes move out of the capillary at the arterial end due to the diffusion gradient as these substances are used in cells

↓

As the blood moves to the venous end of the capillary the blood pressure reduces

↓

Water then moves back into the capillary by osmosis

↓

$CO_2$ and other waste products move into the capillary with some fluid

↓

Some fluid drains into the lymphatic system

# Transport of Oxygen

```
┌─────────────────────────────────────────────────────────────┐
│ When haemoglobin is exposed to gradual increasing           │
│ oxygen tensions it is absorbed gradually at first           │
└─────────────────────────────────────────────────────────────┘
                              ↓
┌─────────────────────────────────────────────────────────────┐
│ Then as it increases in tension the oxygen is absorbed      │
│ more slowly                                                 │
└─────────────────────────────────────────────────────────────┘
                              ↓
┌─────────────────────────────────────────────────────────────┐
│ In the presence of carbon dioxide oxygen is released from   │
│ haemoglobin                                                 │
└─────────────────────────────────────────────────────────────┘
                              ↓
┌─────────────────────────────────────────────────────────────┐
│ During high partial pressures of oxygen, oxygen bonds       │
│ with haemoglobin to form oxyhaemoglobin                     │
└─────────────────────────────────────────────────────────────┘
                              ↓
┌─────────────────────────────────────────────────────────────┐
│ In low partial pressures of oxygen it dissociates from the  │
│ haemoglobin                                                 │
└─────────────────────────────────────────────────────────────┘
                              ↓
┌─────────────────────────────────────────────────────────────┐
│ When partial pressures of carbon dioxide are high, the      │
│ haemoglobin is more efficient at dissociating with oxygen   │
│ than associating with it                                    │
└─────────────────────────────────────────────────────────────┘
```

**FLOW DIAGRAMS**

# Chloride Shift

Carbon dioxide diffuses into a red blood cell

↓

The $CO_2$ bonds with water in the presence of carbonic anhydrase to form carbonic acid

↓

This carbonic acid immediately splits into $H^+$ and hydrogen carbonate ions ($HCO_3^-$)

↓

The $HCO_3^-$ diffuses out into the plasma and combine with sodium ions to form sodium hydrogen carbonate

↓

This induces the diffusion of $Cl^-$ ions into the red blood cell to balance the electrochemical gradient

↓

The $H^+$ now present triggers the dissociation of oxygen from haemoglobin

↓

The haemoglobin acts as a buffer when haemoglobin combines with the $H^+$

↓

The dissociated oxygen then moves out of the red blood cell into the tissues

# Setting up a Potometer

```
A leaf shoot is cut under water
            ↓
The apparatus should be completely filled with water, with
no air bubbles
            ↓
The leaf shoot is then fitted to the rubber tubing under
water
            ↓
The potometer and shoot is then removed from the water
            ↓
The leaves are dried and joints sealed with waterproof
jelly
            ↓
An air bubble is then introduced into the capillary tube
            ↓
The distance the air bubble moves in a given time is
measured
            ↓
To repeat the measurement the air bubble is moved back
to the start using the water reservoir
```

FLOW DIAGRAMS

# Translocation & Mass Flow

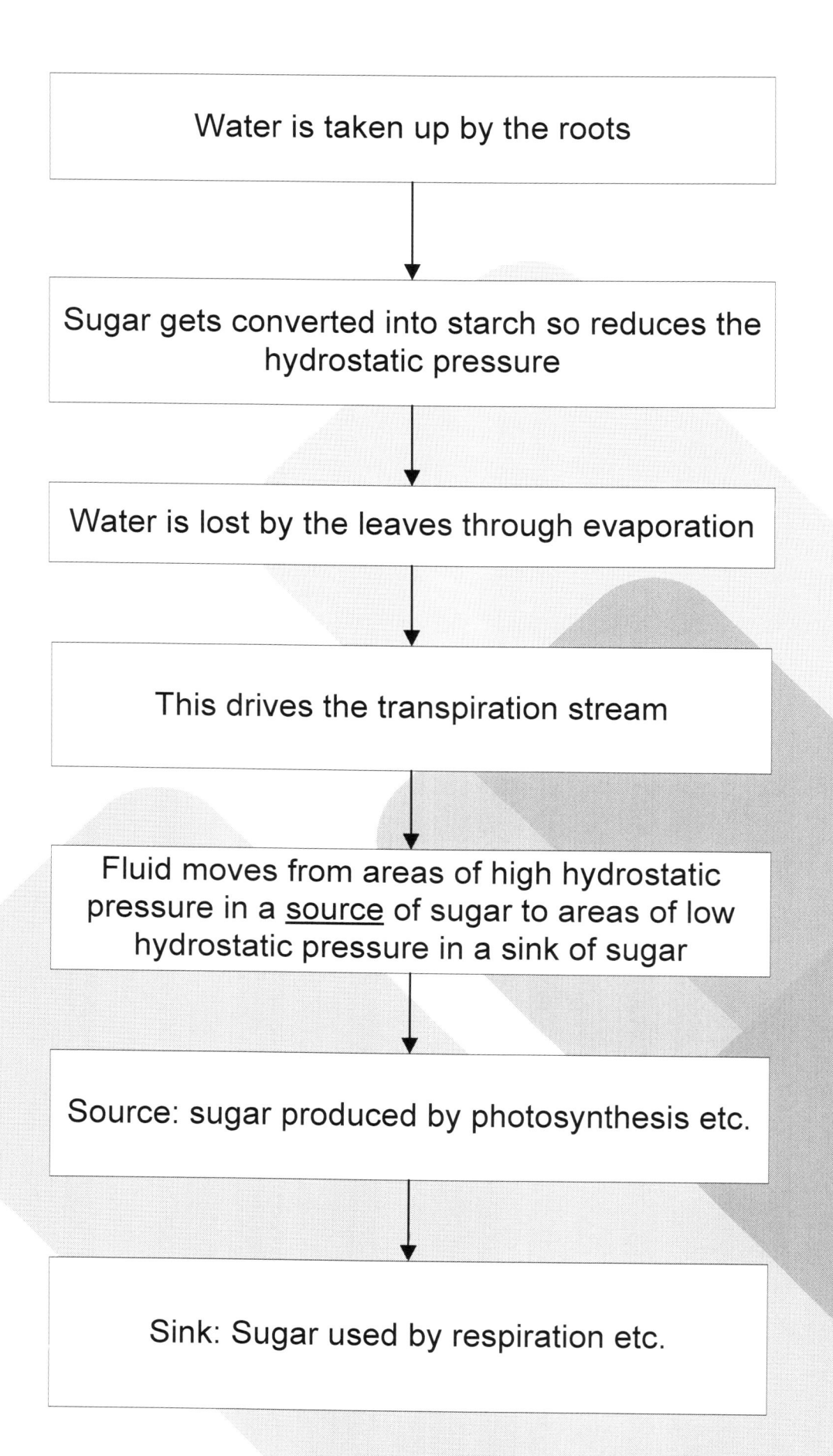

```
Water is taken up by the roots
          ↓
Sugar gets converted into starch so reduces the hydrostatic pressure
          ↓
Water is lost by the leaves through evaporation
          ↓
This drives the transpiration stream
          ↓
Fluid moves from areas of high hydrostatic pressure in a source of sugar to areas of low hydrostatic pressure in a sink of sugar
          ↓
Source: sugar produced by photosynthesis etc.
          ↓
Sink: Sugar used by respiration etc.
```

# Memory Spider Diagram Topics

Here you will find a list of the key topics in the module. For each of these topics you can construct memory spider diagrams every couple of weeks to track the progress of your knowledge.

To do this, take a piece of paper and put the title of the topic in the middle of the page in black pen.

Then, without the aid of any text books or your notes, in black pen write down everything you can remember about that topic.

Once you cannot remember anymore, find the chapter concerning that topic in your text books and notes and look up the information that you missed.

In red pen add the missed out material to your spider diagram.

Keep your spider diagram for your records and use it to compare to subsequent diagrams that you construct on the same subject to show the proportion of black to red and see how you are progressing.

# Memory Spider Diagram Topics

- Microscopes
- Organelles
- Prokaryotes & Eukaryotes
- Cell Membranes & Communication
- Transport Across Membranes
- New Cells
- Stem Cells & Meiosis
- Cell Specialisation
- Tissues
- Lungs
- The Heart & Circulation & Blood Vessels
- Blood, Tissue Fluid & Lymph
- Carriage of Oxygen & Carbon Dioxide
- Transport in Plants

# Answers

All the answers to the basic questions and linked topic questions can be found in this section.

# Microscopy

1. - Magnification - This describes how much larger an image is than the actual object. The image size divided be the actual size of the object
   - Resolution - The degree that it is possible to distinguish between two different objects. With a higher resolution, more detail will be seen.
2. This involves adding a coloured chemical to the specimen. The chemical bonds to the specimen and allows the specimen to be seen more clearly.
3. The specimens are placed in wax and allowed to harden, they are then sliced into sections so that different parts of the specimen can be seen.
4. Eyepiece magnification x objective lens magnification.
5. - Human eye - 100 micrometers
   - Light microscope - 200 manometers
   - Electron microscope - 0.20 nanometers
6. The microscope will contain or can be fitted with a small ruler called an eyepiece graticule. This can be calibrated using the magnification to work out the actual size of the specimen.
7. The stage micrometer is 1 mm long and contains 100 divisions which are 10 micrometers apart. It is then possible to calculate the value of one eyepiece division using the magnification being used. E.g. If the eyepiece lens is x10 and the objective lens is x4 the total magnification is x40. This mean 40 epu = 1000 micrometers. So 1 epu is 1000 divided by 40 = 25 micrometers for each single division.
8. Image size divided by Magnification.
9. A beam of electrons is focussed by magnets onto the specimen and passes through it, producing an image on photographic film.
10. Scanning electron microscope - The electron beam does not pass through the specimen, but are reflected off and a 3D image is produced.
    Transmission electron microscope - The electron passes through the specimen and gives a 2D image.
11. Advantages - They have a much greater resolution than light microscopes, therefore more detail can be seen. With the scanning electron microscope a 3D image is produced, giving extra detail of the specimens.
    Disadvantages - The electron beam must be directed toward the specimen in a vacuum, therefore the specimen must be dead before it can be prepared. The electron microscopes are large pieces of equipment and are highly expensive. The preparation of specimens is much more complex than that of light microscopes.
12. This allows distinction between different objects to be seen more clearly.
13. Similarities - They both magnify small specimens so that more detail can be seen. The specimens must be prepared before being viewed.
    Differences - The electron microscope specimen must be dead, but the light microscope may view live specimens. More resolution with the electron microscopes. The light microscope is less expensive and easier to use.

# Cells and their contents

1. A structure contained within individual cells which carry out specific functions.
2. This is the structure of a cell as shown be an electron microscope, so that all the detail is shown.
3. - Cytoskeleton - adds stability to the structure of cells, provide movement for cells.
   - Flagella - have the same structure as cilia, they contain many mitochondria to produce ATP to allow their movement. This enables specialised cells such as sperm to move around.
   - Vesicles & Vacuoles - these are surrounded by a membrane and are capable of transporting different substances within them, they can also provide structure as in plant cell vacuoles.
   - Plant cell walls - this gives plants cells their rigid structure and aids with the overall structure of the plant as a whole. They are made of strands of cellulose which make them strong. With the aid of a full vacuole (turgid cell) the plant cells are kept full and keep their shape.
4. What are the structures and functions of the following:
   - Nucleus - The largest organelle of the cell and contains genetic material in the form of chromatin. The nuclear envelope holds the chromatin in the nucleus, but contain pores in order for some molecules to pass through. The nucleus also contains a small spherical structure called the nucleolus. The chromatin contains the genetic material unique to the organism and codes for all the different proteins of the organism. This ultimately controls the cell and thus the organism, as within different cells, different protein are activated, giving them a specialism.
   - Endoplasmic reticulum - This is a membrane bound organelle, which has been flattened into sacs known as cisternae. There are two types, rough ER which holds ribosomes on its outer membrane and smooth ER which does not. Rough ER is the site of translation in protein synthesis, and then transports the proteins away. Smooth ER is involved in lipid synthesis.
   - Golgi apparatus - This is also a membrane bound organelle that has been flattened into sacs. The sacs sit on top of one another. The protein from the rough ER are modified by the Golgi apparatus and then packaged into vesicles and transported to their destination.
   - Mitochondria - This is an ellipsoid shape, with a double membrane, the inner of which is folded and called cristae. The central fluid filled part of the mitochondria is known as the matrix. The mitochondria is the site of aerobic respiration, during which ATP is created. This provides energy for all active processes within the organism.
   - Chloroplasts - These are only found in plant cells as they are the site of photosynthesis, when light is harvested to produce carbohydrates for respiration. They have a double membrane and contain stacks of flattened sacs called thylakoids, which join to form the granum. The inner space is known as the stroma.
   - Lysosomes - A single membrane spherical sac. Enzymes are contained within the lysosomes which are applied to break down certain substances, such as pathogens within a phagocytic white blood cell.
   - Ribosomes - They are made of two sub units which come together during translation of protein synthesis to manufacture proteins.
   - Centrioles - Protein fibres made into tubes and are used in the cell division process.

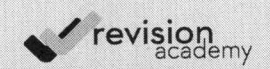

5. A gene is a section of bases on a DNA strand that codes for a particular protein. The strands of DNA coil together to make a chromosome,
6. - A copy of the coding gene is made in the nucleus and produces an strands of mRNA.
   - This moves out of the nucleus into the cytoplasm of the cell.
   - A a ribosome either free in the nucleus or attached to rough ER the protein is synthesised.
   - The protein is then sent to the golgi apparatus and modified and packed into a vesicle. The vesicle is now transported to its destination either within the cell or the vesicle fuses with the cell membrane and the protein is released outside of the cell.
7. Prokaryotic cells have more of a basic structure than eukaryotic cells. They do not contain membrane bound organelles and their genetic material is free within them. They have a cell wall, where as only plant eukaryotic cells have a cell wall. The production of ATP within a prokaryote occurs at a mesosome. Most prokaryotes are associated with diseases. Their ribosomes are much smaller than that of eukaryotic cells, and the cells as a whole are generally smaller than eukaryotic cells.
8. Prokaryotic cells are used in food production and many are found in the guts of mammals and aid with digestion.
9. Eukaryote.
10. - Hydrophobic - when a molecule is repelled by water moves away from water molecules.
    - Hydrophilic - when a molecule is attracted to water and moves towards it.
11. They allow the movement of molecules to be controlled between two different regions.
12. Contains a phosphate, hydrophilic head and hydrophobic fatty acid tails.
13. This makes up the basic structure of plasma membranes and is made of two layers of phospholipids
14. Molecules with no charge do dissolve in water and are known as soluble particles and charged molecules are insoluble.
15. As phospholipids contain hydrophobic tails, when placed in water, the tails orientate themselves away from the water and a bilayer is formed with the fatty acid tails arranged on the inside, protected from the water by the hydrophilic heads.
16. Cell membranes of muscle have many channels so that glucose is readily taken up by the cells so that ATP production is not impeded. Plasma membranes contain channels and cell signalling protein for communication between cells and other substances that are unable to pass through the membrane.

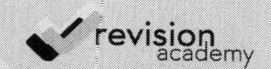

# Membranes & Transport

1. Allows some solutes and water to pass directly through the membrane.
2. This is the theory of the structure of cell membranes, containing a phospholipid bilayer and allowing proteins embedded within it to move around slightly.
3. Phospholipid bilayer, carrier and channel proteins either spanning the whole membrane (intrinsic) or embedded in one layer (extrinsic). Cholesterol, glycolipids, glycoprotein.
4. A phospholipid with an attached carbohydrate molecule.
5. A phospholipid with an attached protein molecule.
6. What do the following do in membranes:
   - Cholesterol - adds stability and structure to the membrane
   - Channel proteins - allows larger and charged molecules to diffuse across the membrane
   - Carrier proteins - to allow molecules to be pushed against a concentration gradient across the membrane, or for specific molecules to move via diffusion.
   - Receptor sites - these are involved when substances are unable to pass through the membrane, but are still able to pass information into the cell, also for cell signalling.
   - Enzymes and Coenzymes - these are involved in the metabolic processes of the cell.
7. Temperature provides energy for movement in the form of kinetic energy. This can disrupt bonds between molecules and eventually rupture membranes as the bilayer is no longer able to hold its shape.
8. Communication between different cells within an organism.
9. Recieves the hormone insulin and allows changes within their target cells which allow more permeability to glucose and as a result there is a reduction in glucose within the blood.
10. Medicine molecules are complimentary in shape to receptors on the cell surface membrane.
11. Some viruses bind to cell membrane receptors and enter the cell and damage genetic material, other block receptors so that the cells cannot recieve messages from other molecules.
12. Movement energy.
13. Diffusion - when substances move along a concentration gradient, from an area of high concentration to an area of low concentration until equilibrium is reached across a membrane without the use of proteins.
    Facilitated diffusion - acts the same as diffusion but is for charged and large particles, so channel and carrier proteins help to move the molecules across the membrane.
14. Steroid hormones are lipid based and able to pass directly through the phospholipid bilayer via diffusion. Glucose is a large molecule, and therefore must travel through a protein molecule.
15. Temperature provides energy for movement in the form of kinetic energy. With a high temperature, molecules are moving faster and so the diffusion rate is faster. Having a greater surface area for molecules to pass through, decreasing the pathway for diffusion and increasing the concentration gradient all aid to increase the rate of diffusion.

16. By their charge and size, and if their specific protein carrier/channel is present.
17. When energy from ATP is used to force substances to move against a concentration gradient from and area of low concentration to an area of high concentration.
18. Through endocytosis into the cell in vesicles and exocytosis out of the cell also in vesicles.
19. Calcium ions being pumped into muscle cells when they relax.

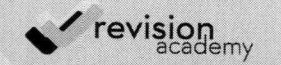

# Water

1. The movement of water molecules from an area of relative high water potential to an area of relative low water potential across a partially permeable membrane.
2. - Solute - a substance that is able to dissolve.
   - Solvent - the liquid that dissolves a solute.
   - Solution - The solute and solvent combined.
3. Water not involved in dissolving the solute.
4. The tendency of water molecules to diffuse from one region to another.
5. Measured in kilo Pascals and the highest value is 0 kPa.
6. If the water potential inside a cell is lower than that of the surrounding fluid, water molecules will tend to move into the cell, and increase the pressure within it.
7. If water potential is higher within a cell than that of the surrounding fluid, water molecules will tend to move out of the cell, decreasing the pressure inside the cell.
8. What happens to cells in solutions of:
   - High water potential - They become turgid or haemolysed.
   - Low water potential - They become crenated or plasmolysed.

# Cell Cycles & Divisions

1. See the flow diagram on page 104.
2. Genetically identical daughter cells.
3. When DNA is combined with proteins called histones.
4. Enzymes move along the DNA checking for any abnormalities.
5. This depends on the species, smaller, more simple organisms cell cycles are much faster than larger more complicated organisms.
6. Daughter cells also require all the functioning organelles that were found in the parent cell, so these must be replicated also.
7. Cell division that produces two genetically identical daughter cells.
8. What happens in each of the following phases:
   - Prophase - Chromosomes shorten and thicken and become visible under a microscope.
   - Metaphase - Chromosomes align themselves on the equator of the cell.
   - Anaphase - Chromosomes are pulled apart and drawn to the two poles of the cell.
   - Telophase - Two nuclear envelopes form, two new nuclei.
9. No, they clone themselves by binary fission.
10. Mitosis occurs in the meristem cells within the meristem of a plant.
11. A genetically identical individual produced from one parent.
12. Cell division similar to mitosis, but involves the genetic material of a prokaryote, which is not in the form of chromosomes.
13. An un-specialised cell that is capable of dividing many times and become any type of cell.
14. See the flow diagram on page 97.
15. When a cell splits in two to form two new cells.
16. Meiosis.
17. Meiosis produces 4 genetically different cells, with half the number of chromosomes, these are used in sexual reproduction.
18. When cells change and become specialised for a particular function.
19. No, ATP is made, energy is released when ATP is hydrolysed.
20. Cells can specialise by changing the number of organelles they contain, changing the overall shape of the cell, or adding extra organelles, for example flagellum in the sperm cell.
21. Erythrocytes lose many of their organelles, including their nucleus and contain a large amount of the protein haemoglobin and are capable of carrying oxygen and carbon dioxide around the body. Neutrophils are white blood cells involved in protecting the organism from disease.
22. They provide the enzymes to break down pathogens that the neutrophil has ingested.

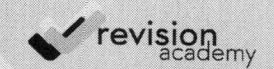

# Organism Organisation

1. - Tissues - a collection of identical cells that are specialised for the same function.
   - Organs - a collection of similar tissues that work together to perform a particular function
   - Organ systems - a collection of organs working together to perform a specific function.
2. Xylem are elongated, waterproof, rigid cells that transport water.
   Phloem, have additional companion cells and transport the products of photosynthesis around the plant.
3. A layered tissue, that is smooth and flat and found in vessels where fluids are transported, such as blood vessels.
4. A layered tissue, made of column-shaped cells, that often produce cilia and mucus.
5. Leaves are thin to allow light to penetrate through their entire thickness. They contain a palisade layer full of chloroplasts for maximum photosynthesis. They have a waxy cuticle to prevent water loss. Small hole, called stomata are present on the lower epidermis, to allow the exchange of gases and water, needed in photosynthesis.
6. Stomata are able to open and close due to the action of the guard cells surrounding them. This allows the leaf to control gas exchange in and out of it,
7. The nervous system instructs the muscular system on when and how to conduct movement.

# Exchange & the Lungs

1. A surface specialised to aid the transport of molecules across it.
2. Organisms require oxygen and glucose for respiration. many other substances are needed to move around the body across surfaces, such as lipids, for fat storage, protein for repair and growth, water and minerals.
3. The lungs act as an exchange surface for oxygen and carbon dioxide. Small intestine, for absorption of nutrients, root hair cells in plants. They must have a large surface area, short diffusion distance, be moist and a high concentration gradient.
4. The lungs consist of rings of cartilage travelling down the throat called the trachea, this then branches off in two directions in tubes called bronchi. The brochi then branch into smaller tubes called bronchioles. At the end of these branches small bulbous sacs called alveoli are found. It is at this point where the gas exchange takes place.
5. The lungs have a large surface area, for many molecules to diffuse across at once. There is a short diffusion pathway for molecules to pass through. There is a steep diffusion gradient. The capillaries in the alveoli are very near the surface to decrease the diffusion distance.
6. Describe the processes of:
   - Inspiration - The diaphragm contracts and flattens. External intercostal muscles contract and the ribs raise. This increases the volume of the chest and the pressure within the lungs drops, drawing air into the lungs.
   - Expiration - The diaphragm relaxes and pushes up. External intercostal muscles relax and the ribs fall. This decreases the volume of the chest and the pressure increases forcing air out of the lungs.
7. The only difference the trachea and bronchi have is their sizes. The bronchi are much narrower than the trachea. They both contain cartilage, elastic fibres and smooth muscle.
8. Complete the following table:

| Tissue | Role |
|---|---|
| Smooth Muscle | Able to contract and constrict the airway, this controls the amount of air reaching the alveoli and ensuring they do not burst. |
| Elastic fibres | The elastic fibres reverse the effect of the smooth muscle and widen the airway. |
| Goblet cells & glandular tissue | These secrete mucus which coats the airway. The mucus traps particles of dust and pathogens that are drawn into the lungs. |
| Ciliated epithelium | These contain cilia which are used to remove mucus that has trapped foreign material, and this is moved to the mouth where it can be swallowed into the stomach and destroyed. |

9. Move air in and out of the lung cavity.
10. Breathing is the physical process of bringing oxygen into the body and removing carbon dioxide. Respiration is the metabolic process of producing ATP from oxygen and glucose.

11. Tidal volume - this is the volume of air that moves in and out of the lungs with each breath.
    Vital capacity - Is the largest volume of air that can move in and out of the lungs.
    Residual volume - This volume of air always remains in the lungs to prevent the lungs from collapsing.
    Dead space - the air that fills the trachea, bronchi and bronchioles, not involved in gas exchange.
    Inspiratory reserve volume - The amount of air taken in during a deep breath.
    Expiratory reserve volume - The amount of air breathed out during a deep breath.
12. A spirometer is a large chamber filled with oxygen which floats on a tank of water. A person breathes through a mouth piece with their nose closed and takes in the oxygen from the chamber. This causes the top of the tank to fall. When the person then breathes out the tank raises. The rise and fall of the container are recorded by a data logger.

# Transport in Animals

1. With larger surface area to volume ratios, organisms need less of a transport system. Larger animals have smaller surface area to volume ratios and therefore need good transport systems.
2. Single circulatory system - Blood only flows through the heart once, this means that blood pressure is reduced and the blood will not flow very quickly, therefore reducing the rate of oxygen received by the respiring cells

   Double circulatory systems - Blood travels in two circuits, and flows through the heart twice. The blood is pumped to the lungs to collect oxygen and then pumped again by the heart to the rest of the body. This means that blood pressure is more easily controlled. However, blood pressure has the potential to become to high.
3. See the flow diagram on page 103. The sino atrial node initiates the contraction of the atria, which pushes blood into the ventricles. The atrioventricular node then contracts the ventricles from the base upward to force blood out of the heart. Blood received from the body is deoxygenated. The blood is the oxygenated as it travels through the lungs. The blood is then oxygenated as it travels back to the heart from the lungs and then away from the heart to the body tissue.
4. Blood pressure in the atria is failrly low as blood needs only to travel to the ventricles. The left ventricle has a thicker wall as blood must be pumped to all body tissue, the right ventricle only pumps blood to the lungs therefore has a thinner muscular wall. Pressure is greater in the ventricles than in the atria, as the blood has much further to travel
5. Complete the following diagram of the heart by labelling each part.

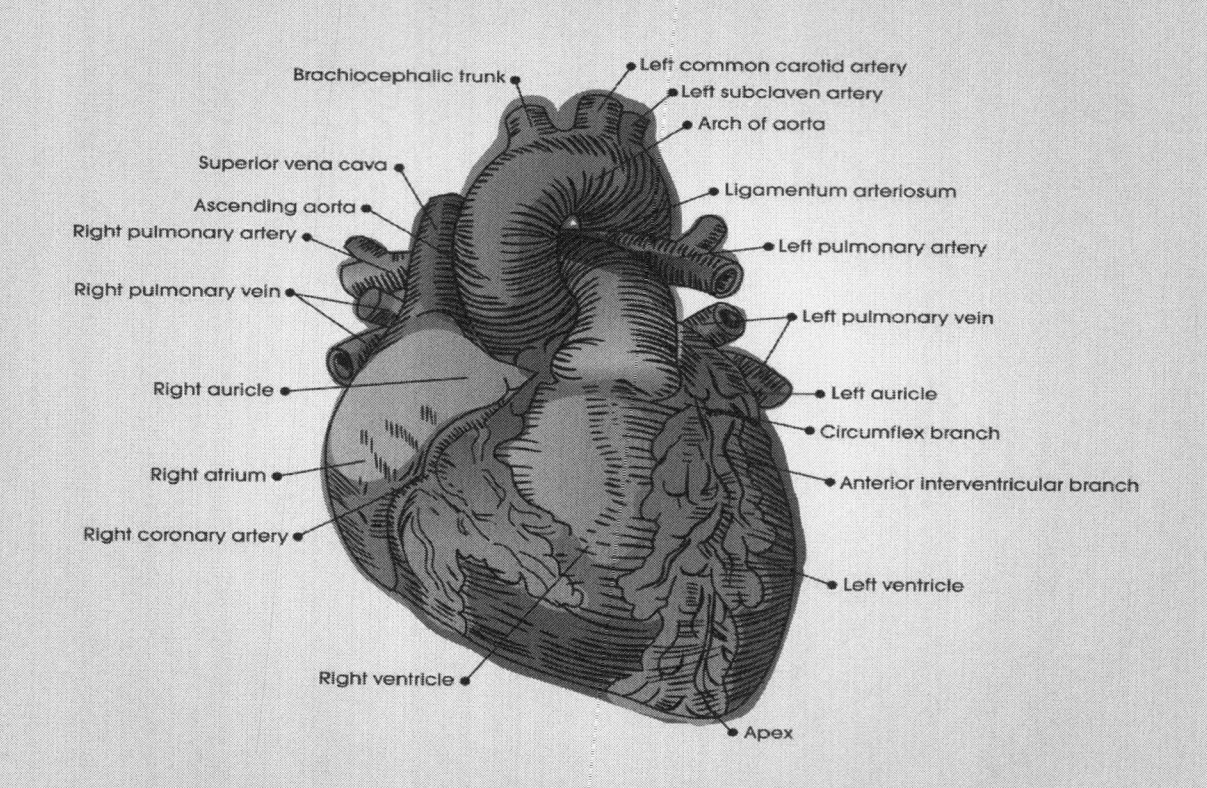

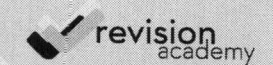

Labels:
- Brachiocephalic trunk
- Left common carotid artery
- Left subclaven artery
- Arch of aorta
- Superior vena cava
- Ligamentum arteriosum
- Ascending aorta
- Right pulmonary artery
- Left pulmonary artery
- Right pulmonary vein
- Left pulmonary vein
- Right auricle
- Left auricle
- Circumflex branch
- Right atrium
- Anterior interventricular branch
- Right coronary artery
- Left ventricle
- Right ventricle
- Apex

6. Blood fills both atria at the same time. The atria contract at the same time, and this increases the pressure within them. The pressure forces the atrio-ventricular valves open and the blood is forces into the ventricles. The blood in the ventricles fill the valve flaps and the valves snap shut.
7. To begin all valves of the heart are shut. Contraction begins at the base of the ventricles during ventricular systole and the pressure increases, this forces the semi-lunar valves open and the blood is forced upwards and out of the heart.
8. Diastole is when the muscles of the heart are relaxed and the heart is filling with blood, systole is when muscles are contracting and pushing blood into ventricles or out of the heart.
9. When the atrioventricular valves are closed they stop back flow of blood from the ventricles into the atria.
10. When the semi-lunar valves are closed they prevent back flow of blood from the aorta and pulmonary artery back into the ventricles.
11. The initial sound of the heart beat is the sound of the atrioventricular valves closing and the second is when the semi-lunar valves are closing.
12. The sinoatrial node sends a wave of excitation across the atria.
13. The electrical impulse from the SAN is received by the muscular tissue of the entire atria and causes the muscle to contract.
14. The atrioventricular node receives the electrical impulse from the SAN, there is a brief pause to allow blood to completely fill the ventricles. The AVN then sends a wave of excitation down the septum through the purkine tissue to the base of the ventricles and causes contraction of the muscle from the base upwards.
15. An ECG shows the electrical activity of the heart. The P wave is atrial excitation, QRS is ventricular excitation and the T section is diastole of the heart beat.
16. Open circulatory system - The blood of the organism is not restricted in vessels and allowed to flood the body cavity, blood is directed to different parts of the organism through movements of the organism.
Closed circulatory system - The blood is contained in blood vessels, creating a higher pressure and a faster rate of flow through the organism. An additional fluid known as tissue fluid bathes the respiring cells.
17. Tissue fluid bathes the respiring cells to allow transport of substances from the blood vessels to the cells.
18. This is a layer of cells that line the inside of a blood vessel.
19. Complete the table about the attributes of arteries.

| Attribute | Structure / Function |
| --- | --- |
| Lumen | Small to maintain high pressure |
| Wall | Thick and contains protein fibres and collagen to withstand the high pressure |
| Elastic tissue | Stretchy to allow the wall to stretch and move with each heartbeat, creating a pulse |
| Smooth muscle | Can contract and restrict the vessel to control blood flow |
| Endothelium | Large surface area that can fold and unfold as artery stretches |

20. Complete the table about the attributes of veins.

| Attribute | Structure / Function |
|---|---|
| Lumen | Larger than an artery, for easy blood flow |
| Wall | Thin walls as blood is under less pressure than an artery |
| Valves | Flaps that prevent back flow of blood |

21. Complete the table about the attributes of capillaries.

| Attribute | Structure / Function |
|---|---|
| Lumen | Narrow to aid gas exchange as red blood cells are squezed as they pass through the vessel |
| Wall | One cell thick to allow a short diffusion pathway for gas exchange |

22. Platelets are small fragments which aid blood clotting, this can be useful when vessels are severed to prevent blood leaking.
23. Pressure in the blood caused by contraction of the heart muscle.
24. See flow diagram on page 106.
25. A lymphocyte is a type of white blood cell found in the lymphatic system which is capable of engulfing pathogens and destroying them.
26. Fluid not returned to the blood vessels during tissue fluid formation drains into the lyphatic system.
27. A globular protein capable of caryying oxygem within red blood cells.
28. Having an affinity means that a substance has an attraction for something else.
29. Dissociation is when haemoglobin is forced to release oxygen.
30. Partial pressure or oxygen tension refers to when there is a mixture of gases, it is the pressure provided by oxygen in that mix.
31. An oxygen dissociation curve shows how readily haemaglobin takes up oxygen at different partial pressure of oxygen.
32. Foetal haemaglobin has a higher affinity for oxygen than adult haemaglobin. This means that faetal haemaglobin can become more saturated with oxygen at lower partial pressures of oxygen.
33. Carbaminohaemoglobin is when haemoglobin combines with carbon in a red blood cell.
34. carbon dioxide is transported in the red blood cells as carbaminhaemaglobin, dissolved directly in the blood plasma, or travels as hydrogencarbonate ions in the plasma.
35. See flow diagram on page 108.
36. Respiring tissues are at a lower oxygen tension than the red blood cells, this will cause oxygen to move to the lower oxygen tension and be released from the oxyhaemaglobin.
37. Hydrogen ions produced as a result of carbon dioxide uptake by red blood cells compete with oxygen for haemaglobin. The presence of the hydrogen ions, dissociates the oxygen from the haemaglobin. With more hydrogen ions, oxygen is more readily dissociated. Therefore with a higher concentration of carbon dioxide (when cells respire more) oxygen is more likely to dissociate and be taken up by respiring cells.

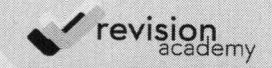

# Transport in Plants

1. Vascular tissue is the tissue that plants use to move water and other substances around it.
2. Xylem vessels transport water and soluble mineral from the root of the plant, upwards to the leaves of the plant.
3. Phloem vessels transport the products of photosynthesis around the plant.
4. Vascular bundles refer to both the xylem and phloem vessels.
5. The endodermis contains the vasuclar bundles, holding them in place.
6. Meristem cells are the cells of the plant found in the meristem where cell division takes place.
7. The pericycle is area of meristem cells within the endodermis.
8. Xylem vessels are situated outside of the phloem vessels in the stem around the edge of the stem.
9. Xylem vessels are long cells that are no longer living and do not contain any organelles. They do not contain end walls and their walls are impreganated with lignin.
10. The empty long xylem vessels allow the ease of water movement through them. The lignin within the vessel walls provides support for the vessels and also waterproffing to prevent water from leaking out of the vessels. The vessels also conatain pits which allow water to leave the vessel and travel to another.
11. Phloem consist of sieve tubes and companion cells. The sieve tubes do not contain a nucleus or much cytoplasm. They have end walls with may gaps to allow dissolved sugars to pass through the cells easily. Gaps called plasmodesmata allow the passage of material from the sieve tubes to the companion cells. The companion cells are true cells with a nucleus and cytoplasm and many mitochondria.
12. Sieve tubes allow the flow of dissolved sugars to travel through them to different parts of the plant.
13. Companion cells carry out the metabolic processes for the sieve tubes and move glucose from photosynthesising cells into the sieve tubes through the plasmodesmata.
14. The tendency of water molecules to move from one region to another.
15. A turgid cell is one that is full of water.
16. Plasmolysis is when water has moved out of a cell and the cell becomes flacid.
17. Water potential of pure water is 0 kPa. Anything with solute dissolved within it, such as cells, will have a negative water potential. Water moves from regions of high water potential (less negative) to regions of low water potential (more negative).
18. Complete the table about movement of water between plant cells.

| Pathway | Description |
|---|---|
| Apoplast | Water moves through the water spaces of the cellulose cell walls |
| Symplast | Water moves through the cytoplasms of the cells and through plasmodesmata |
| Vacuolar | Water moves through the vacuoles of the plant cells |

19. Root hair cells absorb mineral from the soil by active transport and water by osmosis.
20. See flow diagram on page 105.
21. The Casparian strip blocks the apoplast pathway of water and forces water to travel through the cell cytoplasm. It then prevents back flow of water through the apoplast pathway once the water has eneterd the xylem vessel.

22. Root pressure is caused by osmosis of water into the xylem caused by active transport of ions into the xylem vessels, this helps to push water up the xylem vessels.
23. Transpiration pull is created when water evaporates from the plant leaves, this water must be replaced. Water molecules are polar molecules and are attracted to one an other by cohesion forces. This causes water molecules to be pulled up the stem.
24. Cohesion-tension theory is the action of the atraction of water molecules to one another, and their movement due to this.
25. Capillary action involves the attraction of water molecules to the walls of the xylem vessels, known as adhesion. This aids their movement up the xylem vessels.
26. Water leaves the leaf through gaps in the lower epidermis of the leaf called stomata. Water will move out as the water potential outside the leaf is lower than that inside the leaf.
27. Transpiration is the loss of water from a plant through the leaves and upper regions of the plant.
28. Water vapour potential is tendency of water vapour molecules to move from one region to another.
29. The movement of water in a plant allows cells with a constant supply of water to maintain turgidity. Photosynthesising cells require water for photosynthesis. Dissolved minerals within the water are required by different parts of the plant. Evaporation from the leaves can keep the plant cool.
30. If a plant loses too much water, plant cells can become plasmolysed and flacid, thus reducing the stability of the stem and the plant can wilt. In addition, the rate of photo synthesis will also decrease as this process requires a constant supply of water.
31. Complete the table on the factors effecting water loss.

| Affecting Factor | Consequence |
| --- | --- |
| Air movement | Greater air movement reduces the water potential outside the leaf, so transpiration is increased |
| Temperature | Higher temperatures will increase the rate that water is evaporated from the leaves, thus increasing water loss through the stomata and the rate of transpiration |
| Number of leaves | More leaves mean more surface area for evaporation and more stomata for water to be lost from, so greater transpiration |
| Amount of light | Increased light levels will open the stomata to allow gaseous exchange of gases for photosynthesis |
| Stomata | More and large stomata mean graeter water loss rate |
| Availability of water | Less water available in the soil will decrease the rate of transpiration as there is less water to replace what is lost through transpiration |
| Cuticle | This is waterproof and reduces water loss from the leaf |
| Humidity | More humid environments increase the water potential outside the leaf, therefore reducing the rate of transpiration pull |

32. A xerophyte is a plant that has adapted to survive in a habitat with a significantly reduced amount of water available.
33. Xerophytes preven water loss by having smaller leaves to reduce the surface area for evaporation. The plant contains a thick waterproof cuticle, the stomata are controlled more readily, they have the ability to roll their leaves to prevent water loss from the lower epidermis,.

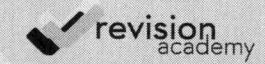

34. Translocation is the transport of products from photosynthesis through the phloem vessels to different areas of the plant.
35. See flow diagram on page 110.
36. A source of sucrose is where sucrose is created through photosynthesis and is loaded into the phloem vessels. A sink of sucrose is where sucrose is used in a metabolic process and leaves the phloem vessels.
37. Where water moves along the phloem, carrying products from photosynthesis, from an area of high hydrostatic pressure to an area of low hydrostatic pressure is known as mass flow.

# Linked Topic Question Answers

1. **How does the structure of a plant cell relate to the structure of a plant as a whole?**
   Cellulose cell wall impregnated with lignin.
   Provides support for each plant cell.
   Many plant cells making up tissue contribute to plant structure and stability, particularly within the stem.
   Permanent vacuoles allow individual cells to become turgid.
   This aids again with structure within the plant.

2. **How does meiosis help to maintain biodiversity?**
   Having different parents with different genes leads to variation.
   Genetic material from a sperm and an egg.
   During Meiosis 1 chromosomes cross over. Crossing over means change in the chromosomes. Chromosomes line up at random along the equator.
   Random assortment means differences in the genetic material of daughter cells.
   This produces variation within organisms.
   Different organisms will be able to survive different selection pressures.
   This helps to maintain the population of each species.

3. **How are microscopes useful to determining information about organisms?**
   Microscopes are able to create a larger image of small parts of an organism.
   This information can be used to help to understand more about the organism.
   This can lead to classifying organisms correctly.
   Knowing more about certain organisms, such as pathogens can be useful to curing disease.

4. **How can the movement of water across cell membranes aid other transport processes?**
   Provides a transport medium.
   Some molecules will be able to diffuse faster as they are able to move around.
   Water will diffuse by osmosis natural down a water potential gradient.
   The movement of water molecules may help larger molecules to move more quickly.

5. **How can measuring lung capacity give an indication of oxygen transport within an individual?**
   Diseases and smoking may affect the lung volume of an individual.
   This may mean that the individuals respiring cells are receiving less oxygen.
   Due to lower concentrations of oxygen entering the body.
   The volume could give an indication on potential issues with the lungs.
   It may help to identify problems before they harm the individual.

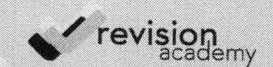

# Acknowledgements

Special thanks to Ben Richardson for proof reading and checking through the workbook.

We would also like to thank Amanda Mann for help with data input.

The author and the publisher would like to thank the following for permission to reproduce the following images:

Cover: Knorre/shutterstock

p.8: DesignPrax/shutterstock

p.12: Synthus design

p.20: Synthus design

p.27: Valdis torms/shutterstock; tan_tan/shutterstock

p.31: Maxi_m/shutterstock

p.38: Synthus design

p.41: Synthus design

p.46: Synthus design

p.49: SumHint/shutterstock

p.60: Synthus design

p.131: dalmingo/shutterstock

p.140: dream designs/shutterstock, Mopic/shutterstock, Creations/shutterstock

# Also in this series.......

**OCR AS Biology Unit 2 Revision Workbook** — 2013/14 Edition
ISBN 978-1-910060-03-2

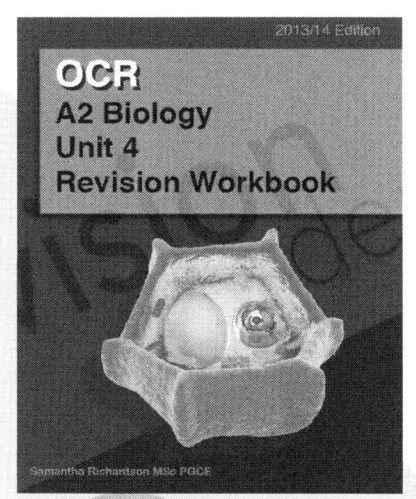

**OCR A2 Biology Unit 4 Revision Workbook** — 2013/14 Edition
ISBN 978-1-910060-00-1

**OCR A2 Biology Unit 5 Revision Workbook** — 2013/14 Edition
ISBN 978-1-910060-01-8

Synthus Publishing

www.synthus.co.uk

revision academy

Printed in Great Britain
by Amazon.co.uk, Ltd.,
Marston Gate.